Principles and Practice of

Planting Trees and Shrubs

Gary W. Watson

E. B. Himelick

Published by
International Society of Arboriculture
P.O. Box 3129
Champaign, Illinois 61826-3129 USA

ISBN: 1-881956-18-0

The ISA seal is a registered trademark

Production Editor: Nancy Komlanc

Graphic Designer: Judy Henderson

Cover Designer: Doug Burnett

Illustrators: Lloyd L. LeMere and Nancy Bartels

Printed by:
United Graphics, Inc.
2916 Marshall Avenue
P.O. Box 559
Mattoon, IL 61938

International Society of Arboriculture

Web Site: http://www.isa-arbor.com

e-mail: isa@isa-arbor.com

10 9 8 7 6 5 4 3 2

1500-PC-4/99

Contents

Preface

Appropriately planted city streets, parks, industrial grounds, and residential areas provide a landscape that increases in value over the years and provides many benefits. To create a functional and beautiful landscape, one must have knowledge of plant materials with training and experience in their use.

Establishing a living landscape that will thrive and increase in value depends on the careful selection and placement of plants, correct planting practices, and adequate maintenance to assure establishment and growth through maturity.

To acquire training in this field, students need a reference that describes transplanting procedures and the research behind them. Landscape contractors, nurserymen, and municipal and commercial arborists follow detailed guidelines when developing specifications for a planting contract. It is intended that this publication serve as a reference for developing more uniform planting procedures.

Acknowledgements

A 1943 publication entitled **Transplanting of Trees and Shrubs in the North-eastern and North Central United States** was published by the National Shade Tree Conference. It was prepared by a committee of several nationally recognized arborists and horticulturists. A second committee prepared a revision published in 1958. In 1981 the publication was rewritten by E. B. Himelick and entitled: **Tree and Shrub Transplanting Manual**. It was published by the same organization under its present name, The International Society of Arboriculture. The two revisions in 1988 and 1991 were reviewed by several plant professionals throughout the United States.

Many plant professionals throughout the United States provided constructive review comments at many stages during the preparation of this book. The authors are grateful to the following reviewers for their contributions: Keith Warren, J. Frank Schmidt & Son Co.; Jim Urban, Urban & Associates; Larry Costello, University of California, Davis; James Martin, Capizzi & Co.; Philip Rodbell, Massachusetts Department of Environmental Management; Edward Gilman, University of Florida, Gainesville; Kirk Himelick, Longwood Gardens; Bonnie Appleton, Roger Harris, Virginia Tech; Cinda Baley, Equisystem; Christopher Dunn, Patrick Kelsey, George Ware, The Morton Arboretum, Tom Perry, Natural Systems Associates; Tim Thornhill, Pawling Properties Associates; Roger Kjelgren, Utah State University; Mike Arnold, Texas A&M University; and Sandy Clark, Village of Mount Prospect, Illinois.

Introduction

Previous editions of this book have been called the *Tree and Shrub Transplanting Manual*.[1] Transplanting involves digging a plant from one site, then replanting it in a new location. Many nursery plants today are grown in containers. Technically, these plants are not transplanted. The scope of this revision has been broadened to include more information on container grown trees and shrubs. To reflect this change, the more general term *planting* has been used in the title in place of *transplanting*.

This book is intended to help landscape professionals and gardeners alike to successfully plant trees and shrubs. Information on the biology of the plants during planting and establishment at the new site constitute the *principles* of planting. Information is included that will help the reader to develop a basic understanding of how the transition to a new environment affects plants. Knowledge of the basic principles involved will be useful when encountering circumstances that are not directly addressed in this book. As much information as possible is presented, even if some of the cited research or observations may currently be somewhat debatable and in need of additional confirmation.

The *practice* of planting is addressed by providing text and illustrations with very practical information that can be put to immediate use. Simple planting procedures that could be performed by anyone are discussed in detail. General information about more highly specialized procedures and equipment is presented briefly in order to help the reader understand the processes, but the discussion is not intended as a comprehensive step-by-step description of procedures that are best performed after thorough training or by qualified contractors.

Planting large trees, small trees, and shrubs is similar in many ways. The need for proper plant selection and site preparation is the same. All plants need careful maintenance after planting in the landscape. The differences between planting trees and shrubs are primarily related to size. It is easy to dig a generous planting hole for a seedling tree or small shrub without much effort. Digging the same relative size hole for a larger tree requires much more effort, and shortcuts are often sought. Larger plants will not establish as fast at the new site and will

---

[1]Published in 1981, revised in 1988 and 1991, by the International Society of Arboriculture.

need special care for a longer period to protect the larger investment. Much of the text of this book naturally focuses on trees because they are larger, more difficult to move. The same principles and practices apply to smaller plants.

Many arborists and horticulturists recognize that at least 80 percent of landscape plant problems originate below ground. Most of these root and soil problems could be minimized or avoided completely through proper selection and planting. Planting on a site that is not properly prepared will result in increased stress for the new plant. A plant that is not well matched to its site will have a shortened life span, sometimes dramatically shortened. It is also important to remember that some sites are not capable of supporting a tree at all.

Section 1

Matching Plants to Planting Sites

The first step in successful transplanting is selecting an appropriate species or cultivar for the planting site. This can be a more complex task than is first apparent. First, you must know the site conditions, above- and below-ground. It is important to answer the following questions:

- What type of soil is present?
- Will there be a lot of de-icing salt used on nearby paved surfaces in the winter?
- How much root space is there?
- Is there potential for damage to nearby structures or pavements from roots?
- Are there nearby utilities, either underground or overhead?
- Will there be root competition or herbicide use associated with turfgrass?
- How much sun and wind exposure will the plant receive?
- Is there potential for vandalism?
- Will low limbs or falling fruits be a problem for passing pedestrians or vehicles?
- Will pesticide spraying be possible if ever necessary?
- What level of maintenance can be expected?

Once you determine the constraints of the site, then you must find trees and shrubs with appropriate qualities. Aesthetic qualities are important but are secondary to ecological qualities that will determine whether the plant will survive on the site. Urban conditions are often quite different than those outside the city.

Native plants from the local region may not be as well suited for an urban site as selections of the same species with more distant origins in somewhat harsher climates that are more similar to the local urban landscape conditions. Native species are not always best for urban sites because conditions are so different. It is also important to select those species and cultivars known to be free of serious disease and insect problems. Tough plants are needed for tough places. By choosing the right plant for the right place your chances of success will be excellent.

chapter

1

Planting Site Evaluation

Before you can choose the right plant, you must know the attributes and limitations of the planting site. The quality and quantity of soil available for root growth and the characteristics of the above-ground environment will influence the size and species of plant that will be able to grow on the site.

IMPORTANT SOIL PROPERTIES

Soil conditions frequently limit planting success. Poorly drained, clay soils, typical of many modern urban developments, require planting procedures much different than those required for well-drained, friable (crumbly) soils found in undeveloped areas and in some older neighborhoods. Trees and shrubs can often be planted with minimal effort and great success in the soils of older neighborhoods. In new developments, site preparation must be much more extensive to achieve the same degree of success. Trees and shrubs may never be vigorous, or long-lived, when planted on very highly disturbed sites. For a more thorough discussion of urban soils see Craul (3).

Topsoil and subsoil

These are terms commonly used, but usually not well defined. A quality topsoil should have:

- silty loam texture (maximum 27 percent clay)
- granular structure
- high organic matter (approximately 5 percent by weight)
- good water percolation and aeration
- moderately high water-holding capacity

- high nutrient content
- no herbicides or other contaminants.

Subsoil, by default, is of lesser quality and the transition can be very abrupt, particularly in a modified soil where a thin layer of topsoil has been spread after the land was developed. The subsoil should permit good drainage, but this is often not the case.

Soil texture

Soil *texture* is the ratio of particle sizes (sand, silt, and clay) in a soil (Figure 1-1). Sandy textured soils are composed mostly of larger particles (0.5-2.0 mm). They are loose, easy to work, readily permit water and air percolation, and have low water holding capacity. These characteristics can result in a rapid breakdown of organic matter and the loss of some plant nutrients through leaching.

Clay soils contain many microscopic particles (<0.002 mm) and have characteristics opposite of sandy soils. Water is held tenaciously, resulting in slow drainage; air exchange is slow, resulting in slow decomposition of organic matter; and some plant nutrients may be tightly bound to the clay particles. Clay soil is easy to compact, often making root penetration difficult.

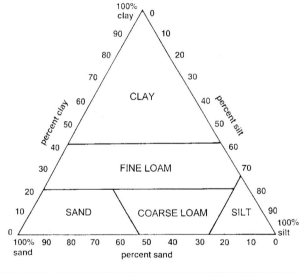

	CLAY	SILT	SAND	COARSE LOAM	FINE LOAM
Air space	low	low	high	moderate	moderate
Drainage	very slow	slow	rapid	moderate	moderately slow
Infiltration	very slow	moderately slow	rapid	moderately rapid	moderately slow
Compactability	high	very high	low	moderate	moderately high
Nutrient capacity	very high	high	low	moderate	moderate
Tilth	poor	poor	good	very good	good

FIGURE 1-1. The soil texture triangle. USDA Classification (Patrick Kelsey 1997).

Silty soils are intermediate between those of sand and clay. Silty soils can also be compacted and poorly drained. When the particles of sand, silt, and clay are in such proportions that the properties of no one group predominate, the soil is called a loam. In these soils, the excessive porosity of sand and the undesirable compactness of clay are favorably modified. Figure 1-2 describes how to determine soil texture by feel.

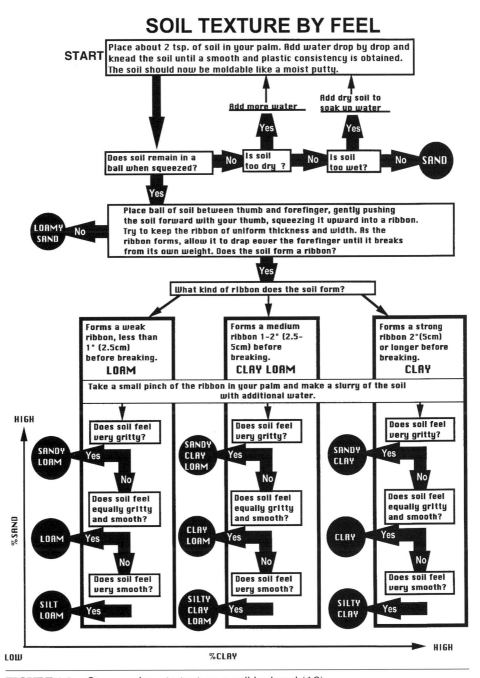

FIGURE 1-2.   Steps on how to texture a soil by hand (10).

Soil structure

The term *structure* refers to the manner in which the soil particles are arranged or grouped together. These groups are called aggregates and can be of many sizes and shapes. Spaces between aggregates allow movement of air and water through the soil and this is also where the roots grow. Well-aggregated soils provide optimum air and water movement through the soil. Poorly aggregated soils are common in developed landscapes, and are often the result of compaction. Organic compounds hold the soil particles together in aggregates. Incorporating organic materials, such as compost, into soils with high clay content, along with proper cultivation, can help to encourage aggregate formation, making them more suitable for planting (Figure 1-3).

Soil contains the aggregates and the pore spaces between them. A good soil contains about 50 percent pore space divided equally between small pores (micropores) and large pores (macropores). Water is held in the small pores by capillary action where it is available to plant roots. Gravity drains water from the large pores providing aeration for roots. A sandy soil has many large pores and few small ones. Thus, it has a low water-holding capacity, a high air capacity, and a high percolation rate. In clay soil, the reverse is true. These soils have many small pores and few large ones resulting in a large water-holding capacity, a low air capacity, and a low percolation rate. An ideal soil for plant growth contains about 50 percent solid particles of which 5 percent is organic, 25 to 30 percent small pore space, and 20 to 25 percent large pore space by volume. Such

FIGURE 1-3. When dry, both well aggregated (top left) and poorly aggregated (bottom left) soils may look similar after cultivation. When wetted, the well-aggregated soil "crumbs" hold together (top right), while "crumbs" of the poorly-aggregated soil do not (bottom right).

a soil would have sufficient water-holding capacity, adequate drainage, and good aeration.

Drainage

Urban planting sites are often excessively wet (1,5). In clay soils, many newly planted urban trees and shrubs die when roots "drown" from too much water. Soil wetness and related drainage conditions are controlled by a number of factors including: 1) precipitation, 2) soil texture and structure, 3) permeability, 4) infiltration characteristics, and 5) landscape position. Soils are poorly drained if water ponds on the ground surface, or in the subsoil, for several days or weeks during wet periods. This is especially prevalent in topographically low or flat sites that receive runoff from surrounding areas, even if the slopes are very gradual. Situations like these cause decline in plants not adapted to wet conditions. Poorly drained soils may require artificial drainage and special planting techniques (see Chapter 3).

There is a very easy, practical way to determine if there is adequate drainage. After digging the planting hole, fill it half full of water. If it has been quite dry, the water may soak in rapidly at first, but it will soon begin to accumulate in all but the most well-drained soils. If the water that fills the bottom of the hole has not dropped appreciably after an hour or two, drainage may be a problem, especially during wet seasons (Figure 1-4). A more accurate measurement can be made by refilling the hole the following day and measuring the drop in water level; a drop of 0.1 in (3 mm) per hour is slow and 5 in (12 cm) per hour is rapid.

FIGURE 1-4.   If water does not drain readily from the planting hole, excess water may drown the roots of a tree planted in the hole.

SOILS AND PLANT GROWTH

The readiness with which the mineral constituents of soil are available to plants depends on at least five chemical and environmental factors of the soil: temperature, water, aeration, nutrient availability, and soil reaction or pH.

Temperature

Favorable soil temperature is needed for bacterial action, movement and absorption of water and nutrients, and root growth. The extent of soil warming depends on the average daily air temperature, the intensity of the sun's rays, and the ability of the soil to absorb heat. The degree to which the sun's rays will heat the soil depends upon how much water is in the soil. Therefore in early spring, well drained soils tend to warm more readily than soils saturated with water. The removal of heavy mulches in the spring will also speed up the soil-warming process.

Water

Water has several functions in plants. Most of the water absorbed by the roots moves through the plant quickly and is released in the atmosphere as vapor through the stomata of the leaves. In the process, dissolved nutrients are moved within the plant and evaporation helps to cool the leaves. Small amounts of water are used in the biochemical processes within plant cells.

Not all water in the soil is available to plants. Some water that is bound hygroscopically to soil particles is held so tightly that the roots cannot extract it. Gravitational water rapidly seeks a lower level in the soil and is gone from the root zone so quickly that it is of limited importance to plant growth. Water held in the micropores by capillary action is held tightly enough to be present in the root zone for extended periods, yet loosely enough for the plant to extract it. The proportion of hygroscopic, capillary, and gravitational water depends on soil texture and structure.

The maximum amount of capillary water a soil can hold, after the gravitational water has percolated through, is called field capacity. Field capacity is when water available to plants is at its maximum.

Aeration

The importance of soil aeration cannot be overemphasized. Plant roots require both moisture and air for normal development. Overwatering or adding water too frequently to heavy clay soils creates a waterlogged condition. Compaction reduces air space and compounds the problem. With the exclusion of air, roots are killed and cannot take up moisture causing desiccation of foliage. As a result, drowning plants often exhibit the same leaf symptoms as those in drought. Trees and shrubs killed by too much water are found most frequently in compacted clay soils.

Plant roots and the soil microflora continually use oxygen and give off carbon dioxide which can be toxic at elevated levels. Thus, a continued exchange of gases between soil and air must take place if carbon dioxide is to be replaced by oxygen.

Nutrients

Plants should be fertilized based on a demonstrated need. The need for fertilization must be determined by a soil test or visible deficiency symptoms in the plants. Growth of newly planted trees and shrubs is more likely to be limited by water than by nutrients (12,13,14).

The nine essential elements needed in relatively large quantities are oxygen, carbon and hydrogen plus the macronutrients. The seven essential elements needed in small quantities are the micronutrients.

Macronutrients	Micronutrients
• nitrogen	• iron
• phosphorus	• manganese
• potassium	• copper
• calcium	• chlorine
• magnesium	• zinc
• sulfur	• boron
	• molybdenum

Carbon, hydrogen, and oxygen come from the atmosphere or from soil water. Three macronutrients, nitrogen (N), phosphorus (P), and potassium (K) are available in most soils but not always in sufficient quantity to permit optimum growth. Calcium, magnesium, sulfur, and most micronutrients are usually available in most soils and do not often limit plant growth.

Of all the nutrients, nitrogen deficiency most often limits plant growth. Most soil nitrogen comes from decomposed plant material as it is broken down by soil microorganisms. Plants without mulch are more likely to require more frequent supplemental fertilization than plants that are mulched. The nitrate form of nitrogen leaches through the soil easily and may need to be added once the new root system is partially established. Some forms of fertilizer must also be converted in the soil. An unusually cool, wet, or dry spring can cause some species to produce pale, green foliage initially. This condition is usually alleviated when the soil becomes more favorable for nitrogen conversion by soil bacteria.

A sufficient amount of phosphorus is often available, but in some soils, additional quantities may be needed for optimum growth. Soils deficient in phosphorus may result in poor twig and leaf growth in the spring and delayed flower production. Both phosphorus and potassium move very slowly in the soil, phosphorus more slowly than potassium. A potassium deficiency often produces no visual symptoms on most plants other than indirectly reducing growth. Palms growing in potassium deficient soils develop yellow spots or flecks on the leaves.

Soil pH

Soil acidity and alkalinity is referred to as soil reaction, or pH. A pH of 7.0 is neutral. The pH numbers below 7.0 indicate acid reactions with increasing acidity as the number decreases. Numbers above 7.0 indicate alkaline reactions with increasing alkalinity as the number increases. The pH scale is a logarithmic scale with a 10-fold difference between units. A pH of 9.0 is 10 times more alkaline than a pH of 8.0 and 100 times more alkaline than a pH of 7.0.

Soil reaction, or pH, is a general indicator of nutrient availability. In slightly acid to neutral soils (pH between 5.5 and 7.2), most nutrients are available at optimal levels. Some nutrients, such as iron and manganese, become less available in alkaline soils (pH above 7.2) because of chemical changes caused by the alkalinity. Other nutrients become less available in highly acid soils (pH less than 5.5).

Species vary in their ability to tolerate alkaline soils. Many plants that require acid soil also require well-drained soil. In areas of high rainfall, acid soils are usually well drained. Selecting a plant species adapted to existing soil conditions is preferable. Permanently changing the pH of field soil is usually not practical and is frequently impossible. However, some short-term adjustments in pH can be achieved. Applications of lime can raise soil pH. Aluminum sulfate and sulfur can help to lower pH. Changing the pH will take time, but the pH can be raised more quickly than it can be lowered. Ammonium sulfate can also be used if nitrogen application is needed along with pH reduction. Ammonium sulfate may be as effective as aluminum sulfate, but neither are as effective as granular sulfur (11). Tables 1-1 and 1-2 provide recommended levels of materials to add to the soil to change pH. If aluminum sulfate is used, the amount recommended is often twice the amount recommended for sulfur application. Aluminum sulfate may cause injury to some plants, particularly broadleaf evergreens, when high rates are used. The injury is believed to be caused by excessive aluminum.

AVAILABLE ROOT SPACE

Just as a potted plant can grow too large for the volume of soil in the pot, so can a landscape tree reach a size where its growth becomes limited by the available root space. When the root system cannot increase in size anymore because the rooting space is full to capacity, the crown growth will slow but not stop (2,15). Gradually, the size of the stagnant root system becomes proportionately smaller relative to the size of the slowly expanding crown. Water stress becomes more frequent and severe which can make plants more susceptible to secondary disease and insect problems. Because of this, trees in small planting pits grow more slowly and have a shortened life expectancy (Figure 1-5).

TABLE 1-1. Amount of lime needed per 1,000 sq ft (93 sq m) to raise the pH of three soil types.

From pH	To pH	Sandy loam pounds(kg) lime	Silt loam pounds(kg) lime	Silt-clay loam pounds(kg) lime
6.0	6.5	23(10.5)	41(18.6)	58(26.4)
5.5	6.0	23(10.5)	41(18.6)	55(25.0)
5.5	6.5	46(21.0)	83(37.7)	115(52.3)
5.0	6.0	46(21.0)	83(37.7)	115(52.3)
5.0	6.5	69(31.4)	124(56.4)	173(78.6)

TABLE 1-2. Amount of sulfur needed per 1,000 sq ft (93 sq m) to increase the acidity of silt loam soil. Soils high in calcium carbonate may require higher rates.

From pH	To pH	Pounds Sulfur	Kg Sulfur
8.0	7.0	20	9.1
8.0	6.5	30	13.6
8.0	6.0	40	18.2
7.5	7.0	18	8.2
7.5	6.5	20	9.1
7.5	6.0	35	15.9
7.5	5.5	50	22.7
7.0	6.5	15	6.8
7.0	6.0	20	9.1
7.0	5.5	25	11.3
6.5	5.5	25	11.3
6.5	5.0	40	18.2
6.0	5.5	40	18.2
6.0	5.0	30	13.6

FIGURE 1-5. Both trees were planted at the same size, and at the same time. The more restricted root space of the tree on the left slowed the growth of the tree.

The variables to be considered when determining how much root space a tree needs are:

- How large the tree is expected to grow
- How much evaporation and transpiration is expected
- How often the tree will receive rainfall or irrigation
- The kind of soil present

As a general guideline, if above- and below-ground environmental extremes are not severe, the root space should be approximately 2 cu ft of soil for each square foot of crown projection area (8,9). In other words, the soil that is capable of supporting vigorous root growth should be 2 ft (60 cm) deep in the area that will be within the dripline (branch spread) of the mature tree. Of course, length, width, and depth dimensions of the root space can be adjusted where necessary to provide an equal soil volume in a different configuration. Watering will be required more often for trees in a confined root space than it would be for trees with root systems that can spread further, especially during dry periods. Trees growing in light soils and very hot or dry climates will require more soil volume. Cool, moist climates may permit the use of less soil volume.

How can very large trees growing in seemingly small spaces be explained? The most likely explanation is that the roots have "broken out" of confinement and have obtained a source of water and nutrients some distance away. Roots sometimes grow through narrow spaces, up to 100 ft or more with very little branching, until they reach an area of quality soil. The roots may also be growing in nearby sewer pipes which have an ample supply of nutrients and water.

ABOVEGROUND SITE LIMITATIONS

Heat islands

The average summer temperatures in the city can be 5° to 9°F (2° to 5°C) warmer than those in the surrounding suburbs — a phenomenon called heat islands. City centers can be especially hot because buildings, asphalt, and concrete that absorb and store heat comprise 70 to 90 percent of the spaces around plants. Large-scale aspects of the urban environment are only part of the aboveground site evaluation process.

Microclimates of landscape sites can differ widely over short distances. The amount of sunlight a plant receives, and the time of day the sunlight is received, can limit the kind of plant that can be used. An area with morning sun and afternoon shade often produces adequate sunlight early with protection during the hottest part of the day. A location like this may be suitable for species adapted to moderate environments. An area with morning shade and direct sun during the hot afternoon hours may be more suitable for plants that are tolerant of heat or drought stress. On downtown streets shaded by very tall buildings, trees may receive direct sunlight for only a short time at midday on north-south streets, and perhaps none at all on east-west streets. Buildings of any height close to the pedestrian sidewalk on the south side of an east-west street often shade the pavement all day and prevent the sun from helping to melt the snow and ice on the sidewalk. As a result, trees in planting pits on the south side of the street may be subject to higher levels of deicing salt than those on the north side of the street where sun can help to melt snow and ice (6).

Locations on the south side of buildings surrounded by pavements may be exposed to sweeping winds and full sun, reflected light from building surfaces and reflected heat from surrounding pavements. In contrast, on the north side of the same building, the plants may never receive direct sunlight and the associated heat. It is not uncommon for both locations to receive the same amount of water from a timed irrigation system, subjecting the south side plants to drought stress, or the north side plants to waterlogging. Proper plant selection and good management practices are both important for vigorous healthy plants.

Air borne pollutants

Air pollutants cause injury primarily to foliage. Conifers are generally more affected than deciduous plants. In northern cities, the most serious airborne pollutant is usually deicing salt used on roadways. Both salt water droplets and dry salt dust particles are dispersed into the air by high-speed traffic. Salts cause plant damage by drawing moisture out of the tissues. Salt deposited on twigs can cause dieback and witches-brooming (Figure 1-6) (4). Sensitive plants can be damaged up to 1,240 ft (378 m) away from a high-speed highway (7). Highly

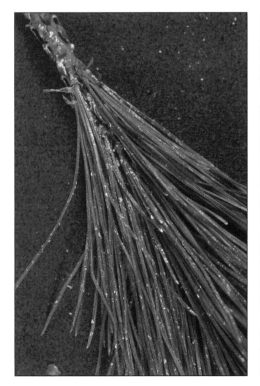

FIGURE 1-6.   Deicing salt accumulates over the winter on branches and needles (left) and can cause witches brooming on a deciduous tree (right). (photo credit P. Kelsey)

susceptible species should not be planted near major roads that are frequently salted. Ocean salt spray can also cause damage in coastal areas (Figure 1-7).

High levels of soil salts can dehydrate plant roots and cause desiccation of the entire plant. When the salts are translocated to the shoots, it can cause marginal leaf scorch, twig dieback, and witches brooming (4). Salt deposited on the soil will usually flush away with the spring rains unless drainage is inadequate.

Knowing the attributes and the limitations of each planting site is imperative for choosing the right plant. Only then can a plant be chosen that has the ability to survive, and thrive, on the site.

FIGURE 1-7. Ocean salt spray deposited more heavily from the left side caused the asymmetrical shape of this tree. (photo credit - J. Patterson)

LITERATURE CITED

1. Berrang, P., D.F. Karnosky, and B.J. Stanton. 1985. *Environmental factors affecting tree health in New York City.* J. Arboric. 11:185-189.
2. Boland, A.M., P.D. Mitchell, I. Goodwin, and P.H. Jerie. 1994. *The effect of soil volume on young peach tree growth and water use.* J. Amer. Soc. Hort. Sci.119: 1157-1162.
3. Craul, P.J. 1992. Urban Soils in Landscape Design. John Wiley & Sons, Inc. NY. 396 pp.
4. Dobson, M.C. 1991. De-icing salt damage to trees and shrubs. Forestry Commission Bulletin 101, HMSO, London. 64 pp.
5. Gilbertson, P. and A.D. Bradshaw. 1985. *The survival of newly planted trees in inner cities.* Arboricultural J. 14:287-309.
6. Kelsey, P. and R. Hootman. 1990. *Soil resource evaluation for a group of sidewalk street tree planters.* J. Arboric. 16:113-117.

7. Kelsey, P.D. and R.G. Hootman. 1992. Deicing salt dispersion and effects on vegetation along highways, pp 253-281. **In** D'Itri F.M. (Ed), Chemical Deicers and the Environment Lewis Publishers, Ann Arbor, MI. 585 pp.

8. Kopinga, J. 1985. Research on street tree planting practices in the Netherlands, pp 72-84 **In** METRIA:5 Proceedings Pennsylvania State University, University Park, PA. 100 pp.

9. Lindsey, P. and N. Bassuk. 1991. *Specifying soil volumes to meet the water needs of mature urban street trees and trees in containers*. J. Arboric. 17:141-149.

10. Lindsey, P. and J. Lichter. (Eds). 1994. Designing and Establishing Successful Woody Landscapes - A Technical Resource Manual. Dept. of Environmental Horticulture, UC Davis, CA. 400 pp.

11. Messenger, S.M. 1984. *Treatment of chlorotic oaks and red maples by soil acidification*. J. Arboric. 10:122-128.

12. Perry, E. and G.W. Hickman. 1992. *Growth response of newly planted valley oak trees to supplemental fertilizers*. J. Environ. Hort. 10:242-244.

13. van de Werken, H. 1981. *Fertilization and other factors enhancing the growth rate of young shade trees*. J. Aboric. 7:33-37.

14. Watson, G.W. 1992. *Tree and shrub fertilization*. Grounds Maintenance, January, 43-46.

15. Williamson, J.G., D.C. Coston, and J.A. Cornell. 1992. *Root restriction affects shoot development of peach in a high-density orchard*. J. Amer. Soc. Hort. Sci. 117:362-367.

chapter

2

Selecting an Appropriate Species

Many trees and shrubs can be used in the landscape, but not every species is suitable for every site. The homeowner is often concerned about how soon a tree will provide effective shade. The municipal arborist must consider whether a particular species will survive parkway planting or require extensive mainte-nance. Other city officials may be understandably concerned that trees and shrubs may block visibility at street corners, be damaged in ice and wind storms, or heave sidewalks and curbing. Utility companies and municipalities are con-cerned that trees and their roots interfere with overhead and underground utili-ties. The majority of problems associated with landscape plants can be antici-pated and prevented in the planning stages. **In some locations, the choice is not what species to plant, but whether a tree or shrub should be planted at all.**

ECOLOGICAL ATTRIBUTES

Adaptability to the climate and soil conditions of the urban planting site is important in the choice of plants. Many indigenous and exotic species will do well in urban parks, campuses, and other open areas. But "tough" trees are required for the "tough" planting places found in more highly developed areas where the microenvironments are often inhospitable for trees (28). Some of the best landscape plants come from difficult sites in nature. In floodplains and swamps, prolonged flooding in springtime and excessively dry soils in summer permit survival of only those trees evolutionarily adapted to a broad spectrum of soil-moisture conditions. Many man-made urban soils are also excessively wet in the spring and very dry in the summer. Adverse sites for trees may also be found in other places. Areas with very shallow clay soils developed over limestone are very similar to some urban soils. Trees found growing in these areas sometimes do well in urban landscapes. A tree from a dry or droughty section of its overall geographic range appears to have better coping capacity for urban sites than does a tree of the same species from a more climatically favorable part of the range. Pioneer species, *i.e.*, those plants that colonize open fields or newly formed land surfaces, usually have the capacity to endure a great deal of environmental adversity and are often successful urban plants. Table 2-1 lists examples of trees that are tolerant of adverse urban environmental conditions.

Some plants have specific soil pH requirements. Rhododendron and mountain laurel, for example, require a highly acid soil. Other plants, such as lilac and redbud, thrive in a slightly alkaline soil. In order to avoid future nutritional problems, plants with specific soil pH requirements should be selected only for areas where soil acidity or alkalinity fall within a suitable range (Table 2-2).

Other physiological traits are also important to consider. In northern cities, plants near roadways may be subjected to heavy use of deicing salts. Some plants are more tolerant of salts than others (Table 2-3).

Where water conservation is important, use plant species that conserve water. Many plant species have morphological and physical characteristics that restrict water loss with special adaptations including stomatal closure, thick leaf cuticles, leaf presentation to reduce direct radiation, and high root-shoot ratios. Unfortunately, many temperate landscape plants are considered "water spenders" that use water inefficiently and continue to transpire large amounts of water after initial stress (18).

In some cities, pollution tolerance may be important. Once again, choose species that are tolerant (Table 2-4). Pollution causes conifers to lose their needles prematurely, and the trees cannot maintain normal photosynthesis levels. When weakened, they may be vulnerable to infectious diseases and attack by secondary pests. Root systems of European beech (*Fagus sylvatica*) exposed to polluted air were smaller than plants grown in unpolluted air, perhaps due to reduced carbohydrate availability (27).

Climatic extremes limit the variety of plants that can be grown in any region of the world. Some southern plants cannot survive cold northern winters. Many northern plants will not survive in the south because of the hot summers, insufficient chilling in the winter, or lack of resistance to pests in another region. Species that occur naturally over a very broad geographic area may consist of several distinct populations, or provenances, with different genetically controlled attributes. A plant from one area may not be able to survive over the entire species range (25).

Plants in continental (inland) climates have to be able to survive larger, more rapid drops in temperature than those in maritime (coastal) climates. In some northern continental climates, winter temperatures can vary from extremes of +80° to -20°F (+27° to -29°C) within 2-3 days, or less. During periods of warmer winter weather, dormant trees may become physiologically active for a short period and then be injured by large, sudden drops in temperature. Extremes in soil temperatures during winter often cause severe root damage to less hardy plants. The duration of periods of low temperature, the amount of soil moisture,

TABLE 2-1. Trees that tolerate adverse urban environmental conditions (19,24,28,29,30).

Scientific name	Common name
Acacia retinodes	Acacia
Acer campestre	Hedge maple
Acer x freemanii	Freeman maple
Acer miyabei	Miyabe maple
Acer negundo*	Box elder
Acer nigrum	Black maple
Acer platanoides	Norway maple
Acer pseudoplatanus	Sycamore maple
Acer rubrum var. drummondii	Drummond red maple
Acer saccharinum*	Silver maple
Aesculus hippocastanum	Horsechestnut
Ailanthus altissima*	Tree of heaven
Betula nigra	River birch
Brahea armata	Mexican blue palm
Bucida buceras	Black-olive
Bursera simaruba	Gumbo limbo
Calodendron capense	Cape chestnut
Casuarina equisetifolia*	Australian pine
Catalpa speciosa*	Northern catalpa
Celtis occidentalis	Hackberry
Conocarpus erecta	Buttonwood
Cocus nucifera	Coconut palm
Crataegus sp.	Hawthorn
Erythrina coralloides	Coral tree
Eucalyptus sp.	Eucalyptus
Ficus sp.	Fig
Fraxinus americana	White ash
Fraxinus pennsylvanica	Green ash
Fraxinus quadrangulata	Blue ash
Fraxinus uhdei	Fresno ash
Ginkgo biloba	Ginkgo, maidenhair tree
Gleditsia triacanthos	Honeylocust
Gymnocladus dioicus	Kentucky coffeetree
Ilex x attenuata	Holly
Juniperus sp.	Juniper
Lagerstroemia (hybrids)	Crape-myrtle

continued

TABLE 2-1.   *cont.*

Scientific name	Common name
Larix decidua	European larch
Ligustrum lucidum	Glossy privet
Lysiloma sp.	Wild tamarind
Maclura pomifera	Osage-orange
Magnolia grandiflora	Southern magnolia
Malus*	Crabapple
Morus alba*	White mulberry
Myrica cerifera	Southern waxmyrtle
Ostrya virginiana	Ironwood
Phellodendron amurense	Amur corktree
Phoenix canariensis	Canary island date palm
Phoenix dactylifera	Date palm
Pinus canariensis	Canary pine
Pinus flexilis	Limber pine
Platanus x acerifolia*	London planetree
Platanus occidentalis*	American sycamore
Podocarpus sp.	Podocarpus
Populus alba var. *globosa**	White poplar
Populus deltoides*	Cottonwood
Pyrus calleryana	Callery pear
Quercus agrifolia	Coast live oak
Quercus bicolor	Swamp white oak
Quercus imbricaria	Shingle oak
Quercus lobata	Valley oak
Quercus macrocarpa	Bur oak
Quercus muhlenbergii	Chinquapin oak
Quercus phellos	Willow oak
Quercus robur	Shingle oak
Quercus shumardii	Shumard oak
Quercus virginiana	Live oak
Robinia pseudoacacia*	Locust
Roystonea sp.	Royal palm
Sabal palmetto	Cabbage palm
Sapindus drummondii	Western soapberry
Schinus molle*	Peruvian pepper tree
Sophora japonica	Japanese pagodatree
Swietenia mahagoni	Mahogany
Tabebuia sp.	Trumpet tree

continued

Scientific name	Common name
Taxodium distichum	Baldcypress
Tilia americana	American linden
Tilia cordata	Little-leaf linden
Tilia heterophylla	White basswood
Tilia platyphyllos	Bigleaf linden
Tipuana tipu	Tipuana
Tristania sp.	Brisbane box
Ulmus alata	Winged elm
*Ulmus americana**	American elm
Ulmus crassifolia	Cedar elm
Ulmus parvifolia	Lacebark elm
*Ulmus pumila**	Siberian elm
Ulmus (hybrids)	Hybrid elms
Zelkova serrata	Zelkova

*Though these species are able to thrive in most urban situations, they may have undesirable traits that prohibit their use in many locations or regions.

TABLE 2-2.   Some common landscape plants and their general soil pH require-ments.*

Scientific name	Common name
Plants Best Suited For Acid Soil	
Azalea sp.	Azalea
Chamaecyparis obtusa	Hinoki false cypress
Chionanthus virginicus	Fringe tree
Cornus florida	Dogwood
Crataegus mexicana	Mexican hawthorn
Cupressus lindleyi	White cedar
Gordonia lasianthus	Gordonia
Grevillea robusta	Silk oak
Ilex verticillata	Winterberry
Jacaranda mimosaefolia	Jacaranda
Kalmia latifolia	Mountain laurel
Leucothoe sp.	Leucothoe
Liquidambar styraciflua	Sweetgum
Pieris sp.	Andromeda
Quercus sp.	Oak (especially pin oak)

continued

TABLE 2-2. *cont.*

Scientific name	Common name
Rhododendron sp.	Rhododendron, Azalea
Symplocos paniculata	Asiatic sweetleaf
Taxodium mucronatum	Montezuma baldcypress
Taxus canadensis	Canada yew
Tsuga sp.	Hemlock
Vaccinium sp.	Blueberry

Plants Best Suited For Alkaline Soil

Acacia longifolia	Acacia
Amorpha sp.	Lead plant
Casuarina equisetifolia	Australian pine
Celtis australis	Mediterranean hackberry
Celtis occidentalis	Hackberry
Cercis canadensis	American redbud
Clematis sp.	Clematis
Cytissia sp.	Scotch broom
Deutzia sp.	Deutzia
Gleditsia triacanthos	Honeylocust
Gymnocladus dioicus	Kentucky coffeetree
Holodiscus discolor	Holodiscus
Hypericum sp.	Hypericum
Indigofera sp.	Indigo
Koelreuteria sp.	Goldenraintree
Kolkwitzia amabilis	Beauty bush
Laburnum x watereri	Goldenchain
Lonicera tatarica	Tartarian honeysuckle
Quercus macrocarpa	Bur oak
Quercus muhlengergii	Chinquapin oak
Philadelphus sp.	Philadelphus
Phoenix canariensis	Canary Island date palm
Platanus x acerifolia	Plane tree
Platanus occidentalis	Sycamore
Robinia sp.	Locust
Syringa sp.	Lilac
Tamarix aff. gallica	Tamarix
Washingtonia robusta	Washington palm

*Some species listed based on recommendations of Martínez and Chacalo (24).

TABLE 2-3.   Ease of transplanting and salt tolerance of common landscape trees.

Scientific name	Common name	Salt tolerance[1]	Transplanting ease[2]
Abies sp.	Fir	I	1-2
Acacia longifolia	Acacia	I	
Acer campestre	Hedge maple	T	2
Acer nigrum	Black maple	N	2
Acer platanoides	Norway maple	T	2
Acer pseudoplatanus	Sycamore maple	I	
Acer rubrum	Red maple	N	2
Acer saccharinum	Silver maple	T	1
Acer saccharum	Sugar maple	N	2
Aesculus sp.	Buckeye	I	2
Aesculus hippocastanum	Horsechestnut	T	2
Ailanthus altissima	Tree of heaven, Ailanthus	T	1
Alnus sp.	Alder	N	1
Amelanchier sp.	Shadblow, serviceberry	I	2-3
Asimina triloba	Pawpaw	I	3
Betula sp.	Birch	T-I	2-3
Carpinus sp.	Hornbeam	N	4
Carya sp.	Hickory, pecan	I	3-4
Casuarina equisetifolia	Australian pine	I	—
Catalpa sp.	Catalpa	I	1
Celtis sp.	Hackberry	N	2
Cercidiphyllum japonicum	Katsura tree	I	2
Cercis canadensis	American redbud	N	2
Chionanthus virginicus	White fringe tree	-	2
Cladrastis lutea	American yellowwood	I	2-3
Clusia rosea	Pitch apple	T	2
Cocos nucifera	Coconut palm	T	1
Conocarpus erecta	Buttonwood	T	4
Corylus sp.	Filbert	N	2-3
Cornus florida	Flowering dogwood	I	3
Crataegus sp.	Hawthorn	N	1-2
Cupaniopsis anacardioides	Carrotwood	T	1
Diospyros virginiana	Common persimmon	I	4
Elaeagnus angustifolia	Russian olive	T	2
Fagus sp.	Beech	N	2-3

continued

TABLE 2-3.   *cont.*

Scientific name	Common name	Salt tolerance[1]	Transplanting ease[2]
Fraxinus sp.	Ash	T	1
Fraxinus quadrangulata	Blue ash	I	2
Ginkgo biloba	Ginkgo, maidenhair tree	I	2
Gleditsia triacanthos	Common honeylocust	T	1
Gymnocladus dioicus	Kentucky coffeetree	I	2
Ilex opaca	American holly	I	2-3
Jacaranda mimosaefolia	Jacaranda	-	2
Juglans sp.	Walnut, butternut	T	3-4
Juniperus sp.	Juniper	T	2
Koelreuteria paniculata	Goldenraintree	T	2
Laburnum x watereri	Goldenchain tree	-	2
Larix decidua	European larch	T	3
Larix laricina	American larch	N	2
Liquidambar styraciflua	Sweetgum	I	2-3
Liriodendron tulipifera	Tulip tree, yellow poplar	N	2
Maclura pomifera	Osage orange	I	1-2
Magnolia sp.	Magnolia	I	3
Malus sp.	Apple, crabapple	*	1-2
Metasequoia glyptostroboides	Dawn redwood	N	2-3
Morus sp.	Mulberry	T	1
Nyssa sylvatica	Tupelo, blackgum, sourgum	I	3-4
Ostrya virginiana	Hophornbeam, ironwood	I	4
Oxydendrum arboreum	Sourwood	I	2-3
Paulownia tomentosa	Paulownia	I	1
Persea borbonia	Redbay	T	2
Phellodendron sp.	Corktree	I	1-2
Picea abies	Norway spruce	N	1-2
Picea glauca	White spruce	I	1-2
Picea pungens	Colorado spruce	T	1-2
Pinus nigra	Austrian pine	T	1-2
Pinus sp.	Pine	N-I	1-2
Platanus sp.	Plane tree, sycamore	I	1
Populus sp.	Poplar	T	1
Prunus serotina	Black cherry	N	2
Prunus sp.	Cherry, plum	I	2-3
Pseudolarix amabilis	Golden larch	-	2

continued

Scientific name	Common name	Salt tolerance[1]	Transplanting ease[2]
Pseudotsuga menziesii	Douglasfir	I	2-3
Pyrus calleryana	Callery pear	I	1
Quercus sp.	Oak	N-I	2-3
Quercus alba	White oak	T	3
Quercus bicolor	Swamp white oak	I	2-3
Quercus imbricaria	Shingle oak	I	2
Quercus laurifolia	Laurel oak	N	1
Quercus macrocarpa	Bur oak	I	3
Quercus palustris	Pin oak	I	1
Quercus phellos	Willow oak	I	1-2
Quercus robur	English oak	T	2
Quercus rubra	Red oak	T	3-4
Quercus velutina	Black oak	I	3-4
Quercus virginiana	Live oak	T	2
Rhamnus cathartica	Common buckthorn	T	2
Robinia sp.	Locust	T	1-2
Sabal palmetto	Cabbage palm	T	1
Salix sp.	Willow	T	1
Sassafras albidum	Sassafras	I	3-4
Sophora japonica	Japanese pagodatree	I	3
Sorbus sp.	Mountain ash	I	1-2
Syringa pekinensis	Peking lilac	T	2-3
Taxodium sp.	Cypress	T	2-3
Taxus sp.	Yew	I	1
Thuja occidentalis	Arborvitae, white cedar	N	1
Tilia sp.	Linden, lime	N	1
Tsuga sp.	Hemlock	N	1-2
Ulmus sp.	Elm	I	1
Ulmus pumila	Siberian elm	T	1

[1]T=tolerant of salt, N=not tolerant of salt, I=intermediate in tolerance or intolerance to either aerosol or soil salt (after 19,23,24).

[2]Rated according to ability to generate new roots and tolerance to stress following transplanting.

1=plants most readily transplanted to 4=plants most difficult to transplant.

*Salt tolerance varies by cultivar.

TABLE 2-4.   Trees that are known to be tolerant to at least one type of air pollution and not known to be susceptible to any other (16,24).

Scientific name	Common name	Tolerant to:
Abies balsamea	Balsam fir	O_3
Acer campestre	Hedge maple	SO_2
Acer platanoides	Norway maple	O_3
Acer rubrum	Red maple	SO_2, O_3
Acer saccharum	Sugar maple	SO_2, O_3, PAN
Ailanthus altissima	Tree of Heaven	HF
Alnus acuminata	Alder	HF
Alnus glutinosa	European black alder	HF
Carpinus betulus	European hornbeam	SO_2
Cornus florida	Flowering dogwood	SO_2, O_3
Elaeagnus angustifolia	Russian olive	HF
Eucalyptus camaldulensis	Eucalyptus	SO_2
Eucalyptus globulus	Eucalyptus	SO_2
Fagus sylvatica	European beech	SO_2
Ginkgo biloba	Ginkgo, maidenhair tree	SO_2
Juglans nigra	Black walnut	O_3
Juniperus sp.	Juniper	SO_2
Ligustrum lucidum	Glossy privet	SO_2
Nyssa sylvatica	Black gum, tupelo, sour gum	SO_2
Persea gratissima	————	O_3
Platanus x *hybrida*	Planetree	HF
Platanus orientalis	Oriental planetree	SO_2
Populus alba	White poplar	HF
Populus deltoides	Eastern cottonwood	SO_2
Quercus robur	English oak	SO_2, O_3
Quercus rubra	Red oak	SO_2, O_3
Quercus rugosa	————	HF
Picea abies	Norway spruce	O_3
Picea glauca	White spruce	SO_2, O_3, PAN
Pinus resinosa	Red pine	O_3
Pseudotsuga menziesii	Douglas fir	PAN
Robinia pseudoacacia	Locust	O_3, HF
Salix babylonica	Willow	HF
Thuja sp.	Arborvitae, cedar	SO_2, O_3
Ulmus parvifolia	Lacebark elm	HF

SO_2=sulfur dioxide, HF=hydrogen fluoride, O_3=ozone, PAN=peroxyacetyl nitrate

and the depth of snow cover all affect the maximum depth to which the soil freezes and the minimum soil temperatures in the root zone during the winter.

Many horticultural references and nursery catalogs refer to the United States Department of Agriculture (USDA) map of hardiness zones to describe the cold hardiness of each plant (Figure 2-1). Similar hardiness zones have been established for Europe (22). The low temperature extremes described are not the only climatic consideration for plants. The same temperature hardiness zone includes Long Island, New York, and central Oklahoma. The extreme winter temperatures may be the same, but winter temperature fluctuations, summer heat, rainfall, humidity, and soil type may be very different. Plants from dry climates may not perform well in areas with similar temperatures and higher humidity, because they lack resistance to fungal diseases commonly found in more humid regions. The maritime climate and cool summers in parts of Europe may cause plants to perform differently than in the hardiness zone with the same winter temperatures in North America. Annual root growth is likely to be much less in European zones 8-10 because of cooler summer soil temperatures.

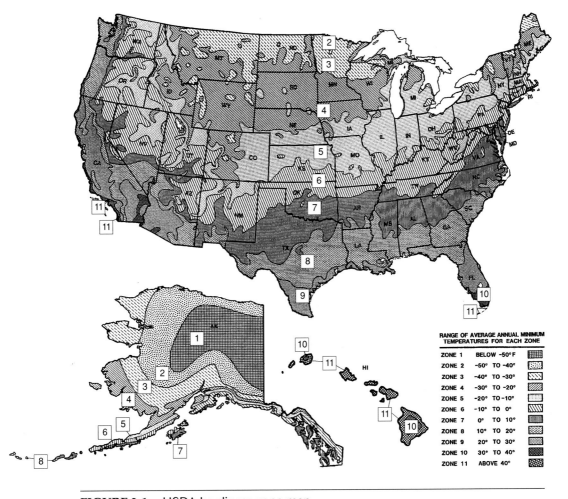

FIGURE 2-1.   USDA hardiness zone map.

Late spring frosts are particularly damaging to those species that break dormancy early, especially when they are planted in areas where they are marginally hardy. If new shoot growth is killed, secondary growth must develop from axillary buds, leading to additional depletion of stored food reserves.

APPEARANCE

The aesthetic qualities of a tree are a major factor in the choice of any plant, and assurance of the aesthetic qualities of the mature plant is important. Plants of the same species grown from seed are not identical. A **cultivar** is a named plant selection from which identical or near-identical plants can be produced. Cultivars are usually selected to exhibit specific desirable aesthetic qualities, such as a special flowering characteristic, a unique growth form, or a more attractive fall color. Many cultivars can be selected from a single species. Some cultivars may be more resistant to insect or disease problems. Cultivars have specific and usually appealing names such as 'October Glory' red maple. Vegetative reproduction or "cloning" is the propagation method most often used.

Many plants have especially attractive features or seasonal interest. Foliage, flowers, fruit, and bark can all add beauty and interest, though not always all on the same plant. Foliage texture and color may not be as spectacular as spring flowers, but can be enjoyed for the entire growing season. Attractive bark can be enjoyed in all seasons. Other characteristics may detract from the usefulness of the plant. Don't make the mistake of considering only a single showy feature. Many crabapple cultivars have beautiful spring flowers, but some also have large, messy fruit that fall later in the season. Apple scab disease can defoliate some crabapple cultivars by mid-summer every year. Hawthorns also have attractive flowers, but most have large thorns that can be dangerous when planted in certain locations.

The question most often asked in relation to tree selection may be "how fast does it grow?" Growth rate is important but should not be the primary consideration when selecting a species or cultivar. Rapid growth usually comes at a price. Many fast-growing trees have other undesirable characteristics such as brittle wood or a short life span. Susceptibility to ice and wind damage are also important factors in tree selection (21).

Longevity is important, but remember that because of site and environmental limitations, urban trees generally have a shorter life span than woodland trees. Thirty to fifty years is considered maximum for many urban trees. Trees in small planting spaces cannot be expected to live even this long. Many fast-growing trees are very short-lived even under the most favorable conditions.

The size, shape, and branching pattern of a tree are important. Low branching, spreading trees are not appropriate along streets but are very useful when screening is desired. Upright selections of trees are quite useful beside buildings and along streets, but look out of place in large open spaces such as golf courses and parks. Tall trees may be hazardous when planted under utility wires, or may look out of proportion near small buildings.

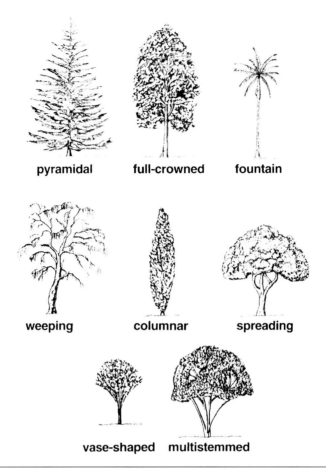

pyramidal   full-crowned   fountain

weeping   columnar   spreading

vase-shaped   multistemmed

FIGURE 2-2.   Tree shape varies widely and is an important consideration when selecting a species.

Where deciduous trees are without leaves for half of the year, the branching pattern becomes a major consideration. A variety of ascending, layered, and weeping branches adds interest in the sometimes uninteresting winter landscape. On a site with many trees, a mixture of plants with attractive summer and winter features is often desirable.

TRANSPLANTABILITY

Plant species vary in transplantability — the ability to generate a new root system and establish quickly at the new site (Table 2-3). Because field-grown plants are often transplanted at least once during production, they usually have a more compact root system and transplant more successfully than uncultivated trees. Root balls of easy-to-transplant species may contain more roots than those of difficult-to-transplant species (20). Large trees are usually more difficult to move than small trees.

Taprooted trees, such as white oak (*Quercus alba*), are often considered difficult to transplant. It is not just the taproot that makes this species difficult. The fine roots are very fragile, and many oak species can be slow to regenerate new roots (17). The procedure for successfully transplanting a difficult-to-transplant species is: 1) sever the taproot at an early age to stimulate greater lateral root development, 2) prune lateral roots for increased fine root development in the root ball, 3) dig a root ball which exceeds minimum standards, 4) prepare a favorable site to encourage new root growth, and 5) provide an extended period of maintenance (especially irrigation in dry weather) since these plants will be slower to establish. **The so-called difficult-to-transplant species can often be moved very successfully if they are moved at the proper time and given the proper preparation and after-care.**

PLANT SIZE

Small trees usually transplant more readily than large trees, although trees 12 to 18 in (30-45 cm) diameter breast height (dbh) measured (4.5 ft (1.4 m) above soil level) are successfully moved by qualified contractors. A few contractors have successfully moved trees of fully mature size.

There are many factors to consider when choosing the best size plant. Some landscape designs require mature trees immediately, dictating the use of large, costly plant material and increased maintenance costs (see Chapter 9). Large trees may not be the best choice for poorly drained sites because the root balls are deeper and more roots could be waterlogged at the bottom of the root ball. In some locations, such as along public sidewalks and streets, very small plant material would not survive due to vandalism. Consider all the factors and make the best choice possible for each situation.

EXPECTED MAINTENANCE

Most plants are susceptible to various kinds of insect pests and diseases, but relatively few are affected to the extent that control measures are required. Seek advice from professionals who are knowledgeable about the problems in your region. Stress can make plants more susceptible to certain problems (26). It is reasonable to expect to take special measures to protect plants from stress-related problems for the first few years, until they have overcome transplanting stress, but plants not well suited to the site will be perpetually stressed. Choosing varieties known to be pest and disease resistant is always better than being forced to use control measures throughout the life of the plant.

Large trees planted under wires will require regular pruning, as will spreading trees planted in areas where the lowest branches must be continually raised for pedestrian or vehicle clearance. Fruits and flowers may fall and cause a mess or a hazard. Avoid selecting plants with large flowers and fruits where people must walk nearby.

Certain plants have been branded as undesirable for urban situations. While they may have maintenance requirements and other features that render them undesirable for many locations, don't dismiss them categorically. In many urban situations, some of these species are the "survivors." While you may not want to plant silver maples, willows or poplars along narrow city streets, they can be an excellent choice for large open areas around retention ponds or along some sections of interstate highway where the "higher quality" trees struggle to survive.

MARKET CONSIDERATIONS

In many urban areas, 80-90 percent of the planted landscape tree population is composed of only a few species or genera because they were the selections that were the most readily available, the most economical to purchase, and easiest to grow. Nurseries often grow large numbers of such species, which helps to make them popular. It is a cycle that is hard to break.

Planting a wide variety of species in public areas is important so that no single disease or insect problem will destroy a large percentage of the urban tree population. The loss of American elms from Dutch elm disease is an example of how devastating this can be. There are other potentially devastating diseases that could develop among certain tree species. The consumer must be educated to know how to match specific trees with specific sites, otherwise, useful species can get a reputation as "hard to grow." Consumers also need to know which trees and shrubs should **not** be planted because of chronic problems. The growers and retailers have a responsibility not to sell trees that may only live a few years in their region, no matter how attractive they may be to the uninformed buyer.

Unfortunately, the availability of certain species or cultivars in desirable sizes is a controlling factor in making plant selections. The supply of a very popular species may be limited until supply can catch up with the demand. Many potentially useful trees are unavailable at local nurseries because the grower is not convinced that there is a market for them. The additional cost of producing slower growing trees may limit their production if the grower is not sure it will be profitable to produce them. The consumer must demand a wider variety and be willing to pay more for harder-to-grow varieties, and the grower must respond. Contract growing of uncommon species and cultivars by some specialized nurseries is sometimes an option.

Studying the characteristics of plants goes hand-in-hand with analyzing the condition at the planting site. With adequate knowledge of both, it is possible to chose the "right plant for the right place."

LITERATURE CITED

16. Anonymous 1973. Trees for polluted air. USDA Forest Service, Miscellaneous Publication No. 1230. 11 pp.

17. Arnold, M.A. and D.K. Struve. 1989. *Green ash establishment following transplant.* J. Amer. Soc. Hort. Sci. 114:591-595.

18. Clark, J.L. and R. Kjelgren. 1990. *Water as a limiting factor in the development of urban trees.* J. Arboric. 16:203-208.

19. Gilman, E.F., H.W. Beck, D.G. Watson, P. Fowler, D.L. Weigle, and N.R. Morgan. 1996. Southern Trees: an Expert System for Selecting Trees. (CD-ROM). University of Florida, Gainesville, FL.

20. Harris, J.R. and N.L. Bassuk. 1994. *Seasonal effects on transplantability of scarlet oak, green ash, Turkish hazelnut and tree lilac.* J. Arboric. 20:310-316.

21. Hauer, R.J., M.C. Hruska, and J.O. Dawson. 1994. Trees and ice storms: The development of ice storm-resistant urban tree populations. Special Publication 94-1, Department of Forestry, University of Illinois at Urbana-Champaign. Urbana, IL. 12 pp.

22. Heinze, V.W. and D. Schreiber. 1984. *Eine neue kartierung der winterhartezonen fur geholze in Europa.* Mitt. Dtsch. Dendrol. Ges. 75:11-56.

23. Kelsey, P.D. and R.G. Hootman. 1992. De-icing salt dispersion and effects on vegetation along highways, pp 253-281. **In** D'Itri F.M. (Ed), Chemical Deicers and the Environment Lewis Publishers, Ann Arbor, MI. 585 pp.

24. Martínez, L. and A. Chacalo. 1994. Los Árboles de la Ciudad de México. Universidad Autónoma Metropolitana, Azcapotzalco, México, D.F. 35 pp.

25. Santamour Jr., F.S. 1979. *Root hardiness of green ash seedlings from different provenances.* J. Arboric. 5:276-278.

26. Schoeneweiss, D. 1978. *The influence of stress on diseases of nursery and landscape plants.* J. Arboric. 4:217-225.

27. Taylor, G. and W.J. Davies. 1990. *Root growth of* Fagus sylvatica: *impact of air quality and drought at a site in southern Britain.* New Phytol. 116:457-646.

28. Ware, G. 1994. *Tough trees for tough situations.* J. Arboric. 20:98-103.

29. Ware, G. 1996. *In search of tough urban trees.* Am. Nurseryman 184:24-29.

30. Watson, G.W., K. Bachtell, T. Green, E.B. Himelick, P. Kelsey, and G. Ware. 1990. Selecting and Planting Trees. Morton Arboretum, Lisle, IL. 24 pp.

Section
II

Preparing to Plant

Traditional gardeners say that you should always spend ten times as much on the planting hole as you do on the plant itself. This is a very simple way of stressing the importance of site preparation. Roots will only grow vigorously where the conditions are favorable. If the site evaluation has revealed poor soil conditions, the only way to assure that the new plant will be able to establish and grow vigorously on the site is to provide adequate site preparation. In confined urban areas, this could be a real challenge . . . and expense.

Spring and fall are the traditional planting seasons, but modern methods and equipment have extended planting into all seasons. Each season has its advantages and limitations. The decision on when to plant is often based on non-horticultural factors, including business pressures and customer demands. The season chosen for planting may have an influence on what kind of plants can be used.

The way in which the plant was produced is also important. High quality, locally grown nursery stock will have a better chance of surviving the transplanting process. Production methods vary somewhat with the region. Container-grown plants have different limitations than balled and burlap stock or bare root plants. Learn the merits and constraints of each before you buy.

chapter

3

Planting Site Design and Preparation

Urban planting sites often have soil conditions that can severely restrict root growth. Site preparation must be more intensive on disturbed sites or sites with naturally poor quality soils. Information obtained from a site evaluation is very important in determining the best way to prepare the site for planting. Expectations of future performance are also important. Planting hole preparation can only provide an optimum environment for root growth for a limited time — usually just a year or two. Long-term survival will depend on selecting a species that will be able to tolerate the existing site conditions.

Not every site requires extensive preparation before planting. Just as seeds falling in the forest require no site preparation, planting on similar sites may require little effort beyond digging a hole large enough for the root ball. In fact, when planting under existing large trees, excessive soil digging may cause serious unnecessary damage to the roots of nearby trees (Figure 3-1).

UNRESTRICTED LANDSCAPE SITES

Many residential and commercial landscape sites offer sufficient root space to support adequate growth of a tree for many years. Planting site preparations should focus on providing the highest quality environment possible for initial root growth during the first year or two after transplanting (possibly longer for trees over 4 in (10 cm) caliper). Even in cool northern climates, roots may extend 3 ft (1 m) from the root ball after two years (65). Though it would be desirable to prepare a larger area, in most cases it will not be practical. When shrubs are planted in groups, it is often possible and beneficial to prepare the entire bed.

FIGURE 3-1. Disturbing just a small part of the root system under an established tree can result in loss of a large portion of the root system. Plant smaller trees and shrubs and plant them as far from the trunk as possible. Dig a smaller than normal planting hole, and take care not to cut any major roots.

The planting site should provide an adequate volume of backfill soil suitable for rapid initial root development and should not restrict root spread beyond the planting hole. Ideally, these objectives should be achieved with a minimum of cost and effort.

Planting hole depth

Holes for bare root plants should be both wide enough and deep enough to accommodate the entire root system, with room for roots to spread. The hole diameter should be 1-2 ft (30-60 cm) wider than the root system. For plants with soil balls, the planting hole should be no deeper than the root ball. The root ball must be supported by firm soil underneath to prevent settling. Most new roots will grow horizontally from the sides of the root ball, so compacted soil at the bottom will not substantially affect overall root growth. The depth of each hole must be measured carefully and matched to the root ball that will be placed in it. If the hole is initially dug too deep, add soil to the bottom and tamp thoroughly so that the root ball will not settle.

Planting hole size

Research studies (38,53,65) and the experience of horticulturists and gardeners have shown that plants benefit from larger planting holes. A larger hole means a greater volume of loose cultivated soil for rapid initial root growth. Trees transplanted with a tree spade also benefit from planting hole at least twice the diameter of the root ball (35,56).

Planting hole shape

Digging a deeper planting hole is not an option; widening the planting hole is the only way to increase its size. In many disturbed urban soils, root growth from the bottom half of a 12-18 in (30-45 cm) deep root ball can be reduced by inadequate drainage and aeration. Since the most vigorous root growth is likely to occur near the surface, this is where digging efforts should be concentrated to have the greatest impact on future root development. A hole with sloped or stepped sides uses the majority of the digging effort to excavate surface soils where the roots will grow most vigorously (Figure 3-2). A planting hole that is two to three times the width of the root ball at the surface is optimum for most situations (Figure 3-3). A wide hole for the full depth of the root ball is harder to dig and may not provide any more usable root space if the soil at the bottom is saturated at times. Even very small plants may benefit from a hole with sloped sides (31).

The root ball may contain as little as 5 percent of the original root system. A planting hole only 25 percent greater in diameter than the root ball with vertical sides can hinder plant establishment. The regenerated root system will reach less than 10 percent of its original size in the backfill before encountering the poor quality site soils that can slow root growth. A hole three times the diameter of the root ball with sloped sides will allow the root system to grow rapidly to 25 percent of its original size before being slowed by the poorer quality site soil — enough to avoid extreme stress under normal conditions. The well-aerated surface soil is increased up to ten-fold by the shallow wide configuration (Figure 3-4).

Concerns are occasionally expressed that this "saucer-shaped" hole will collect water and funnel it towards the root ball. On poorly drained sites, if the water level was easily raised in the narrow bottom of the "saucer-shaped" hole, is is possible that roots could be killed. While this is a valid concern in extreme

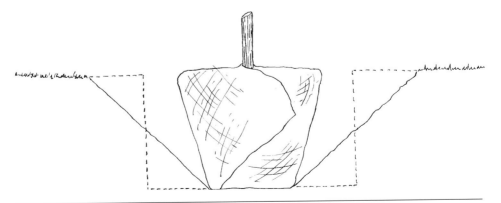

FIGURE 3-2.   The planting hole should be only as deep as the root ball. Compared to a hole with vertical sides of the same volume, a hole with the sloped sides is easier to dig and provides an increased volume of friable soil for vigorous root development from the upper half of the root ball.

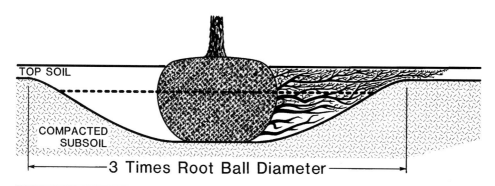

FIGURE 3-3. If roots have difficulty penetrating compacted site soils, sloped sides allow roots to continue to grow vigorously toward the better soils near the surface rather than being trapped in the planting hole. Roots that do penetrate the site soil along the slope will grow more slowly.

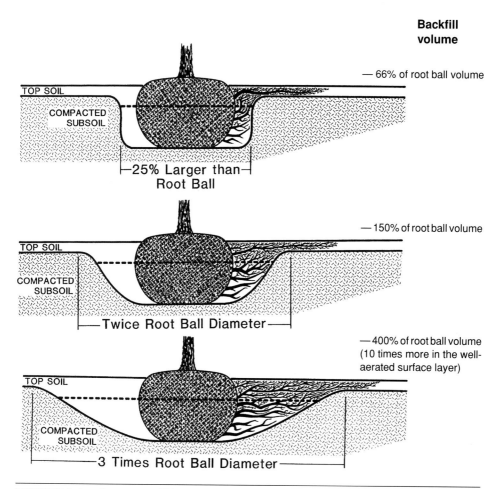

FIGURE 3-4. Amounts of high quality backfill soil provided by several planting hole shapes.

situations, the water would have to rise almost to the surface to cause substantial root injury. When the site is poorly drained, most of the root growth is expected to be in the upper half of the planting hole soil where drainage is better. The upper half of the "saucer-shaped" planting hole contains over 85 percent of the backfill soil. The upper quarter contains approximately 75 percent of the soil in the planting hole. Water could completely saturate the lower 3/4 of the planting hole for extended periods and only affect 25 percent of the root system in the root ball and the backfill soil. If drainage is so poor that excess water could kill the roots in the lower part of the root ball before regeneration can occur, then drainage needs to be corrected.

Ultimately, the roots must spread beyond the planting hole. If the site soil is compacted and difficult to penetrate, the roots may circle inside of the hole, just as they often do inside of a container. If the roots are unable to grow into the compacted subsoil, a hole with sloped sides will allow them to grow back toward the surface soils and continue to spread.

Glazing is a potential problem when digging a hole with mechanical equipment in clay or silty soils. Augers may cause complete and persistent glazing under certain circumstances (32). The sides of the hole should at least be roughened with a hand tool if glazing occurs (54). If the backfill is not going to be amended, it may be more efficient to just break down the sides of the hole after the root ball is in place, creating the much-preferred angled or stepped side (Figure 3-5).

When preparing the wide planting hole, it may not be necessary to remove all the soil and then put it back in the hole. It may be more efficient to first dig a planting hole about 12-18 in (30-45 cm) wider than the root ball. Then after the hole has been backfilled, rototil another 12-24 in (30-60 cm) ring of soil around it as deeply as possible. A heavy-duty tiller with rear tines may be required. A similar procedure can be used for trees moved with a tree spade. Rototil the soil immediately outside the edge of the root ball as deeply as possible, at least two widths of the rototiller. Steering the rototiller in a circle around small root balls may be difficult. When mechanical tilling is not possible, deeply cultivating the

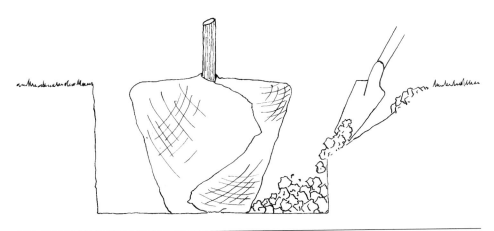

FIGURE 3-5. If planting holes are dug with a large augur, breaking down the sides with a shovel can eliminate glazing and create the preferred sloping side.

soil around the root ball manually after planting may still be more efficient than actually digging a large hole and refilling it.

Backfill soil modifications

Backfill soil amendments are often very controversial. Soil is usually amended by adding organic matter or sand. Is unamended also unmodified? Removing the soil from the planting hole and then backfilling the hole with the same soil **does** modify the soil. The topsoil layer is mixed with the subsoil. Structure is often improved as it is cultivated. The soil is not as compacted when it is returned to the hole as it was before the hole was dug. Unamended is not the same as unmodified.

The interface between backfill soil and undisturbed soil is often blamed for poor root growth into the undisturbed site soil. If the backfill soil is amended, a discontinuity of soil properties may be created between the backfill and site soil. The abrupt change in soil properties may include changes in texture, structure, bulk density, aeration, water movement and availability, color, pH, and chemical composition. Soil water movement may be hindered across the interface between the two soil types, but root growth is often unaffected. Roots can often cross the interface between the backfill and the site soil, but once they do, the poor quality site soil can immediately begin to restrict root extension and growth. In reality, lateral water movement from site soil to backfill soil accounts for only a small part of the water reaching the root system in the root ball and backfill, and the interface may not be of major practical importance.

A study comparing three types of backfills consisting of unamended soil, amended soil, and new topsoil showed that there was no difference in root development in any of the backfills. Root growth in the undisturbed site soils outside of the planting hole was less than root growth in all of the backfill soils including unamended backfill. This was attributed to poorer root growth in the compacted clay site soil after crossing the interface, rather than to an inability of the roots to cross the interface (65). The lack of vigorous root growth in poor site soil beyond the interface is often mistaken to be caused by a restriction at the interface.

Several published research reports indicate that in general, amending the backfill soil with peat and compost may not be beneficial or detrimental to root development or plant growth (37,38,44,46,48,49,55,59,65,66,67). Specific combinations of certain amendments and site conditions have proven beneficial (40,47,55,68) or detrimental (36,58) to plant establishment.

On poor quality sites, backfill soil amendments may be important, but probably not as important as a large planting hole. Organic matter will improve structure, drainage, and fertility in most soils. Well-decomposed organic matter is best. **To insure the best results on sites with heavy clay soils, dig a large hole, then mix equal volumes of soil from the hole, composted organic matter, and sand.** If compost alone is needed, add 5 percent by weight (20-35 percent by volume depending on the material). If sand alone is added, 50 percent or more by volume may be required depending on soil type. If too little sand is added to a clay soil, the mix could be worse than the original soil (60). Test the pH of both the compost and sand. These materials are often alkaline and may not be appropriate for some plants (see Table 2-2). It may be best and more practical to bring in quality topsoil rather than to prepare amended backfill on the site.

Hydrophilic polymer gels have sometimes been shown to be effective when added to the backfill soil. Growth and survival of bare root plants can be improved by gels, especially if subjected to drought (45,57,69), and they can help to extend irrigation cycles (41,61,64,69). Effects are likely to be short-lived because the roots will soon grow beyond the polymer amended backfill.

Drainage

Good water drainage from the bottom of the hole is very important for root regeneration and root penetration into the native soil. Poor drainage accounts for high losses of new plants. Water often drains into the planting hole from the surrounding landscape. The bottom half of the backfill and root ball soil can be waterlogged during wet periods, or if over-irrigated, killing the roots in those soils (Figure 3-6). Excess water from rainfall may only be a problem for part of the year, but even short periods of saturation can cause death of roots of many species. Excessive watering is a frequent factor in planting failure. Irrigation systems designed to provide large amounts of water to lawns also often over-irrigate woody plants. Excess water can easily accumulate in planting holes, even during severe droughts, saturating the soil and driving out oxygen needed by the roots.

Solving drainage problems may be expensive, but it is essential for acceptable plant performance. The need for correcting drainage should be investigated **before** planting (see Chapter 1). Before plans for new developments are approved, adequate drainage from all areas must be provided, but drainage may later be altered by changes made in the landscape. Something as subtle as adding soil to a planting bed can disrupt surface drainage and create a wet area during certain times of the year. Providing adequate drainage to individual trees is often difficult. On many sites, improving the drainage on the entire site may be a better approach. If drainage in a large area requires improvement, regrading or installation of underground tiles may be required.

A layer of gravel in the bottom of the planting hole will not improve drainage. **Gravel in the bottom of the planting hole can make drainage worse, not better.** Water accumulates in the finer textured soil above this layer of coarse gravel until the soil is completely saturated. This is known as a perched water table.

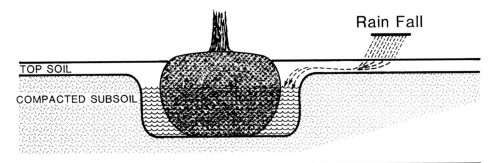

FIGURE 3-6.   Water cannot penetrate compacted subsoil and flows laterally to the lowest point. Planting holes can fill up with water and drown the root systems.

There are several ways to improve drainage for individual trees. A ring of perforated plastic tubing around the root ball in the bottom of the hole connected to a pipe discharging the water at a lower level can be very effective (Figure 3-7, top). A 3 in (8 cm) fall per 100 ft (30 m) of pipe is a minimal slope to obtain adequate water flow. This approach works well for trees planted on slopes. If the ground is level, sometimes permission can be obtained to connect the pipe into a nearby storm sewer.

If a well-drained layer of soil exists underneath a poorly drained layer, then a vertical hole can be drilled through the poorly drained layers and filled with gravel or sand to provide a path for the water to flow away to the well-drained layer (Figure 3-7, bottom).

If the water cannot be drained away to a lower area or a deeper soil layer, it may have to be pumped out of the hole using either the ring of perforated pipe,

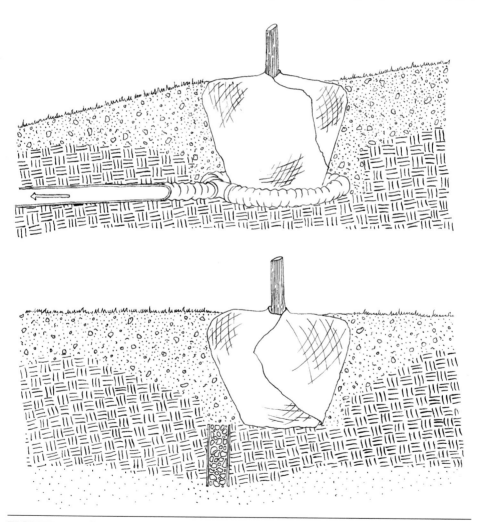

FIGURE 3-7.   Solving drainage problems. A drainpipe can be installed in the bottom of the planting hole if it can exit at a lower point on a slope (top). Drilling a large diameter hole between the bottom of the planting hole and a buried well-drained layer of subsoil can be an effective way of providing drainage (bottom).

or the drilled hole lined with perforated pipe, as a place for water to collect. Hand pumping may be required daily and may not be practical. A small submergible electric pump, such as those used in water features, may be useful in some special situations if a floating on-off switch can be installed.

Another approach to providing improved drainage is to plant the top of the root ball slightly above grade. No more than one-third of the root ball should be above grade, and the soil should be **gradually sloped** between the top of the root ball and the original grade. This method may utilize excess soil from the planting hole or even require additional soil. An important drawback of this method is that the soil in the upper part of the root ball and backfill may dry out quickly during dry periods. A 2-4 in (5-10 cm) mulch layer and more frequent watering during dry periods is recommended.

Low-profile container plants (see Chapter 5) are well suited for poorly drained sites. More of the roots in the wide, shallow root ball will be close to the soil surface where drainage is better. The dimensions of a field dug root ball cannot usually be altered into a low-profile shape.

PLANTING PITS AND PLANTERS

Root space

The limited root space available in planting pits will ultimately limit the size of the tree. When pits are combined and shared by several trees, the performance of the trees seems to be better than when trees are in several smaller individual planting pits (Figure 3-8). The closely spaced canopies of the trees help protect

FIGURE 3-8.   Groups of trees with shared root space in a planter (left) grow larger than single trees in small pits (right). (photo credit - J. Patterson)

each other and the soil from sun and winds. Below ground, roots can spread over a larger area. Though not much additional soil is available for each tree, the larger shared root space provides a more consistent environment for the roots. Soil temperature, moisture, and other factors will be less affected by the container walls.

Soil specifications

When soil volume is restricted, soil quality becomes very important. Too often, trees are planted in whatever soil is present when the pits are created. Whether it is new construction or openings cut in existing pavements, the soil is often of very poor quality and should be replaced. Soils for planting pits and planters should contain (measured by weight) less than 27 percent clay, at least 50 percent medium (1 mm) sand, and 5 percent organic matter (20-35 percent organic matter by volume) (Patrick Kelsey and Phillip Craul, personal communications).

Planting pit design

Traditional planting pits have been openings in the pavement as small as 2 ft (60 cm) square, covered with an open grate. In recent years, the need for larger root spaces has begun to be recognized and better designs have been adopted. A larger pit with a larger grate is a simple way to enlarge the root space, but not always the most effective. Trees need an area of soil that is two ft (60 cm) deep within the dripline of the expected mature size of the tree, or the equivalent in a slightly different shape (50,52).

Many designs provide additional root space underneath the pavement. Planting pits can often be large enough to become shared root spaces, especially for linear plantings along streets. Vaulted systems suspend the pavement above the soil in order to provide an aeration pathway to the soil surface as well as to reduce or prevent compaction of the soil. Drainage and irrigation systems are usually installed as well (Figure 3-9).

Soils designed to support pavement without settling are often called load-bearing soils. To expand planting pits under pavements, the soil must also provide a favorable environment for root growth while supporting the pavement. The first soil of this type was developed in Amsterdam, Netherlands. Amsterdam Tree Soil specifications call for 91-94 percent medium coarse sand, 4-5 percent organic matter, and 2-4 percent clay (by weight). Phosphorous and potassium are added as necessary. The organic matter provides a source of nitrogen (39). The soil mix is carefully compacted to a specific density when installed, and aeration is provided through spaces in the pavers placed over the soil (Figure 3-10). This system has been shown to be effective in providing vigorous trees and stable pavements for many years.

More recently, other load bearing soils have been tested. Usually, large stones are used to create a network of interconnected spaces that can be filled with soil for root growth (43). Testing is still in the early stages in the United States, and engineers must be satisfied with the system before it will be used widely. Similar systems have been used successfully in European countries for several years.

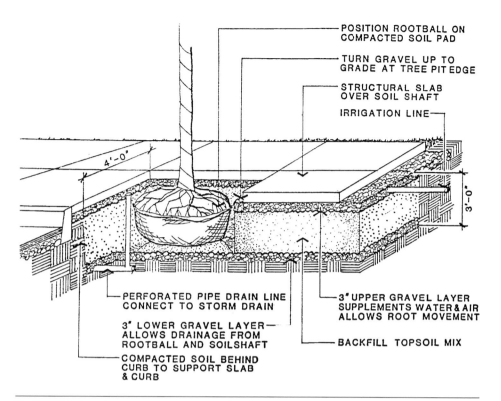

FIGURE 3-9.   Vault systems can provide high quality root space underneath pavements. (Drawing courtesy of J. Urban)

Root barriers

When pavements are laid on a compacted soil base, roots often grow between the pavement and the compacted soil. Roots enlarge and can eventually lift the pavement. Barriers are sometimes installed to force roots to grow deeper. Barriers have been constructed from plastic, metal screening, and geotextile impregnated with herbicide. Most are effective at blocking roots between the surface and the bottom of the barrier. When roots grow under the barrier, they often grow back toward the surface, especially in poorly drained soils (42,62). In well-drained and well-aerated soils, the roots may not return to the surface so quickly, or at all (33,34).

Barriers reduce overall root development of trees (33,42,63). On sites with very poor aeration, the roots may not be able to grow deep enough to go under the barrier. The limited root system on one or more sides could result in poor vigor or instability.

When pavements were laid on a 12 in (30 cm) base of coarse brick rubble or gravel, roots did not grow directly under the pavement (51). The rubble was apparently not a suitable environment for root growth without soil in the spaces in between, and the roots grew in the deeper soil underneath the rubble.

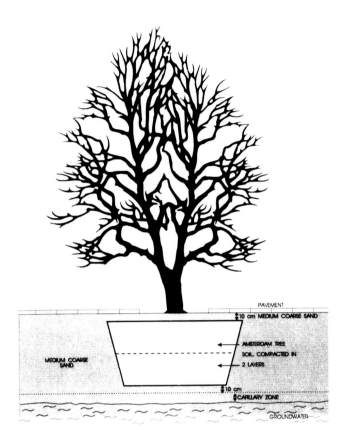

FIGURE 3-10.   Underground tree pit design in Amsterdam. The medium coarse sand surrounding the Amsterdam Tree Soil is compacted to >90% Proctor Density. Note that the tree pit is extended underneath the pavement. (Drawing courtesy of E. Couenberg)

Aboveground planter design

In downtown areas, sidewalks and courtyards may be built over basements, underground parking, or subway systems. In situations like these, trees must be planted in aboveground planters. The decision to plant a tree in a planter must include a permanent commitment for intensive maintenance. The limited amount of moisture held in the extremely small soil volume can be depleted very quickly. Frequent, but monitored, irrigation is required. If the drainage system becomes clogged, excess water will cause damage to roots. Extremes in temperature, especially extremely low temperatures in winter, can cause extensive root injury leading to the death of the plant. The use of larger planters helps to reduce these problems

Planting success depends on good root growth. Good root growth depends on a good quality environment. Without adequate site preparation, the plant will not grow vigorously on the new site and reach its full potential in the landscape.

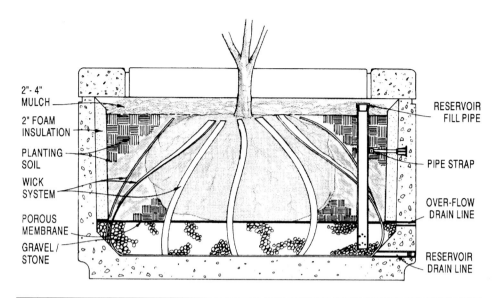

2"- 4" MULCH

2" FOAM INSULATION

PLANTING SOIL

WICK SYSTEM

POROUS MEMBRANE

GRAVEL / STONE

RESERVOIR FILL PIPE

PIPE STRAP

OVER-FLOW DRAIN LINE

RESERVOIR DRAIN LINE

FIGURE 3-11.   Planters designed for the City of Milwaukee provide a water reservoir and wicking system to lengthen the irrigation cycle, drainage to prevent waterlogging, and insulation to minimize temperature extremes. (Drawing courtesy of Wausau Tile, Inc.)

LITERATURE CITED

31. Arnold, M.A. and D.F. Welsh. 1995. *Effects of planting hole configuration and soil type on transplant establishment of container-grown live oak.* J. Arboric. 21:213-218.

32. Auxt, T., S. Blizzard, and K. Elliot. 1980. *Comparison of apple planting methods.* J. Am. Soc. Hort. Sci. 105:468-472.

33. Barker, P.A. 1995a. *Managed development of tree roots. I. Ultra-deep rootball and root barrier effects on European hackberry.* J. Arboric. 21:202-208.

34. Barker, P.A. 1995b. *Managed development of tree roots. II. Ultra-deep rootball and root barrier effects on Southwestern black cherry.* J. Arboric. 21:251-259.

35. Birdel, R.,C. Whitcomb, and B.L. Appleton. 1983. *Planting techniques for tree spade dug trees.* J. Arboric. 9:282-284.

36. Brynes, R.L. 1976. Effects of soil amendments in variable ratios and irrigation levels on soil conditions and the establishment and growth of *Pittosporum tobira*. M.S. Thesis Univ. of Florida, Gainesville, FL.

37. Clemens, J. and S.P. Radford. 1986. *Establishment trials of ornamental trees and shrubs in coastal New South Wales.* J. Arboric. 10:117-123.

38. Corley, W.L. 1984. *Soil amendments at planting.* J. Environ. Hort. 2:27-30.

39. Couenberg, E.A.M. 1993. Amsterdam tree soil, pp. 24-33. **In** Watson, G. and D. Neely (Eds.). The Landscape Below Ground. International Society of Arboriculture, Savoy, IL.

40. Day, S.D., N.L. Bassuk, and H. van Es. 1995. *Effects of four compaction remediation methods for landscape trees on soil aeration, mechanical impedance and tree establishment.* J. Environ. Hort. 13:64-71.

41. Dehgan, B., F.C. Almira, and T.H. Yeager. 1992. *Superabsorbent polymer-amended media for container grown woody ornamental crops.* HortSci. 27:601-602.

42. Gilman, E.F. 1996. *Root barriers affect root distribution.* J. Arboric. 22:151-154.

43. Grabosky, J. and N. Bassuk. 1996. *Testing of structural urban tree soil materials for use under pavement to increase street tree rooting volumes.* J. Arboric. 22:255-263.

44. Harris, R.W., J.L. Paul, and A.T. Leiser. 1977. Fertilizing woody plants. University of California, Davis, Cooperative Extension, Leaflet No. 2958. 23 pp.

45. Henderson, J.C. and D.L. Hensley. 1986. *Efficacy of a hydrophilic gel as a transplant aid.* HortSci. 21:991-992.

46. Hodge, S.J. 1990. *Organic soil amendments for tree establishment.* Arboric. Res. Note 86-90-ARB. DOE Arbor. Advisory & Info. Service, Forestry Commission, UK.

47. Hodge, S.J. 1995. *The effect of seven organic amendments on planting pit soil and tree performance.* Arboricultural J. 19:245-266.

48. Hummel, R.L. and C.R. Johnson. 1985. *Amended backfills: Their cost and effect on transplant growth and survival.* J. Environ. Hort. 3:76-79.

49. Ingram, D.L. and H. van de Werken. 1978. *Effects of container media and backfill composition on the establishment of container-grown plants in the landscape.* HortSci. 13:583-584.

50. Kopinga, J. 1985. Research on street tree planting practices in the Netherlands, pp.72-84. **In** METRIA:5 Proceedings. Pennsylvania State University, University Park, PA.

51. Kopinga, J. 1993. Aspects of the damage to asphalt road pavings caused by tree roots, pp. 165-178. **In** Watson, G. and D. Neely (Eds.) The Landscape Below Ground. International Society of Arboriculture, Savoy, IL.

52. Lindsey, P. and N. Bassuk. 1991. *Specifying soil volumes to meet the water needs of mature urban street trees and trees in containers.* J. Arboric. 17:141-148.

53. Miller, A.N., P.B. Lombard, M.N. Westwood, and R.L. Stebbins. 1990. *Tree and fruit growth of 'Napoleon' cherry in response to rootstock and planting method.* HortSci. 25:176-178.

54. Nicolosi, R.T. 1981. *Influence of backfill and soil density on root growth of urban plants.* New Horizons 1981. pp. 48-53.

55. Pellet, H. 1971. *Effect of soil amendments on growth of landscape plants.* Am. Nurseryman 13:12,103-106.

56. Preaus, K.B. and C.E. Whitcomb. 1980. *Transplanting landscape trees.* J. Arboric. 6:221-223.

57. Savé, R., M. Pery, O. Marfa, and L. Serrano. 1996. *The effect of a hydrophilic polymer on plant water status and survival of transplanted pine seedlings.* HortTech. 5:141-143.

58. Schulte, J.R. and C.E. Whitcomb. 1975. *Effects of soil amendments and fertilizer levels on the establishment of* silver maple. J. Arboric. 1:192-195.

59. Smalley, T.J. and C.B. Wood. 1995. *Effect of backfill amendment on growth of red maple.* J. Arboric. 21:247-249.

60. Spomer, L.A. 1982. Amending landscape soils with sand. Horticulture Facts LH-6-82. Univ. of Illinois Coop. Ext. Serv. 4pp.
61. Taylor, K.C. and R.G. Halfacre. 1986. *The effect of hydrophilic polymer on media water retention and nutrient availability to* Ligustrum lucidum. HortSci. 21:1159-1161.
62. Wagar, J.A. 1985. *Reducing surface rooting of trees with control planters and wells.* J. Arboric. 11:165-171.
63. Wagar, J.A. and P.A. Barker. 1993. *Effectiveness of three barrier materials for stopping regenerating roots of established trees.* J. Arboric. 19:332-338.
64. Wang, Yin-Tung. 1989. *Medium and hydrogel affect production and wilting of tropical ornamental plants.* HortSci. 24:941-944.
65. Watson, G.W., G. Kupkowski, and K.G. von der Heide-Spravka. 1992. *The Effect of backfill soil texture and planting hole shape on root regeneration of transplanted green ash.* J. Arboric. 18:130-135.
66. Watson, G.W., G. Kupkowski, and K.G. von der Heide-Spravka. 1993. *Influence of backfill soil amendments on establishment of container-grown shrubs.* HortTech. 3:188-189.
67. Whitcomb, C.E. 1975. *Effects of soil amendments on growth of silver maple trees in the landscape.* SNA Nursery Res. Conf. Proc. 20:49-50.
68. Wood, C.B., T.J. Smalley, M. Rieger, and D.E. Radcliffe. 1994. *Growth and drought tolerance of* Viburnum plicatum *var.* tomentosum Mariesii in pine bark-amended soil. J. Am. Soc. Hort. Sci. 119:687-692.
69. Woodhouse, J. and M.S. Johnson. 1991. *Water storing soil polymers and the growth of trees.* J. Arboric. 15:27-35.

chapter

4

When to Plant

Planting times are often referred to by season. The seasons indicated on the calendar are determined by the position of the sun relative to the equator. Meteorologists often define the change of seasons a few weeks earlier based on weather conditions. Horticulturists often have a different sense of the seasons based on plant growth. To an avid gardener, spring may begin with the long awaited chance to work in the garden on the first warm day in late winter, but growth of most plants will not begin until the soil warms. To many, autumn may be closely associated with the first frost or when leaf color changes. "Fall" planting may be best shortly after the worst heat and drought stress of summer are past so that roots have plenty of time to grow before the soil cools. There may be several months difference in optimum planting time between regions. The terms "spring planting" and "fall planting" must be interpreted carefully.

Many factors contribute to determining the best time for planting. Experienced gardeners may be able to successfully transplant almost any plant at any time of year by providing intensive attention and care tailored to the specific requirements of each plant. Large-scale commercial plantings often consist of a variety of species with different requirements. Plants requiring less intensive maintenance are often favored. Planting on these sites may have to be restricted to times when plants will require the least amount of care after planting. Plant species and methods of production must also be considered when determining the best season for planting. Factors such as labor and equipment availability, weather and construction delays, and customer demands may dictate planting at the least favorable times of the year, horticulturally speaking. For the greatest chance of success over the widest possible number of situations, many deciduous plants and narrow-leaved evergreens are planted in the fall or early spring when the plants are dormant. Dormant planting reduces demand for soil moisture because transpiration is low. Broad-leaved evergreens are usually planted most successfully in the spring. Important horticultural factors in selecting a planting season are the inherent nature of the species, growth stage of the plant, environmental conditions, transplanting method, and expected level of care after planting.

FACTORS THAT CAN INFLUENCE PLANTING TIME

Horticultural principles play an important part in determining planting time, but horticultural factors may compromise these principles. Many times, non-horticultural considerations result in planting at times that are not very horticulturally desirable.

Horticultural	**Non-horticultural**
• Nature of the species	• Construction schedules
• Growth stage of the plant	• Weather delays
• Environmental conditions	• Plant and labor availability
• Transplanting method	• Budget constraints
• Care after planting	• Customer expectations

NATURE OF THE SPECIES

The inherent nature of the plants selected is extremely important. We continue to learn from experience and experimentation as various plants are planted under different environmental conditions. Plants that do not re-establish readily when transplanted in the fall or winter can often be successfully moved in early spring (Table 4-1). Typical of such species are those having thick and fleshy roots, such as magnolia (*Magnolia*) and tulip tree (*Liriodendron*). Exceptions to this rule occur primarily because of wide variations in climatic and soil conditions.

Plant species vary greatly in their ability to tolerate temperature extremes. Cold-hardy plants are best, of course, but occasionally some of the less cold-hardy exotic species are desired in northern climates to create specific landscape effects, and they must be sited very carefully. Water stress associated with planting is not known to reduce cold-hardiness (70,79), but it may still be best to install plants known to be of borderline hardiness in the spring so that they will be more established before the first winter.

GROWTH STAGE OF THE PLANT

Many plants are transplanted most easily when dormant. The most pronounced state of dormancy corresponds closely with the coldest winter months. Dormancy variations occur between evergreen and deciduous plants. Dormancy is initiated in many plant species at the time of the formation and maturation of terminal buds. Many plants are moved more readily after terminal buds have matured. In general, evergreens can be moved earlier in the fall and later in the spring than deciduous plants. Root growth potential of seedlings increases the longer harvest is delayed in the fall (78,80).

TABLE 4-1. These species are best transplanted in spring.

Scientific name	Common name
Abies sp.	Fir
Betula sp.	Birch
Carpinus caroliniana	American hornbeam
Carya sp.	Hickory, pecan
Cladrastis kentukea	American yellowwood
Cornus florida	Flowering dogwood
Diospyros virginiana	Common persimmon
Fagus sp.	Beech
Ginkgo biloba	Ginkgo
Ilex opaca	American holly
Juglans sp.	Walnut, butternut
Koelreuteria paniculata	Goldenraintree
Laburnum sp.	Laburnum
Larix sp.	Larch
Liquidambar styraciflua	Sweetgum
Liriodendron tulipifera	Tuliptree, yellow poplar
Magnolia sp.	Magnolia
Nyssa sylvatica	Tupelo, black gum, sour gum
Ostrya virginiana	American hophornbeam
Oxydendrum arboreum	Sourwood
Populus sp.	Poplar
Prunus sp.	Cherry, plum
Pseudolarix amabilis	Golden larch
Quercus sp.	Oak
Salix sp.	Willow
Sassafras albidum	Sassafras
Taxodium sp.	Cypress
Tsuga sp.	Hemlock

ENVIRONMENTAL CONDITIONS

Expected weather conditions during the weeks after planting are very important in determining the best season for planting. Temperature and moisture are both important. Extended periods of moderately warm air and soil temperatures, combined with adequate soil moisture, are ideal. Warm, moist soils promote active root growth. Calm air, high relative humidity, and moderate temperatures minimize stress.

The absence of natural soil moisture need not delay planting provided supplemental watering is available at planting and for an extended period after planting. In some tropical and subtropical areas, soils are warm but inadequate rainfall occurs in winter. Fall or winter planting can take advantage of warm soils for root growth and cooler air temperatures for reduced stress as long as irrigation is possible.

In subtropical areas, palms and many other trees can be transplanted year-round though success may be somewhat better in summer. In California and Arizona, however, transplanting palms is more successful during April to September when the soils are warmer and root development is more readily stimulated. Live oaks (*Quercus virginiana*) are usually planted in the fall (October to November) in climates where occasional freezes occur in winter. Growers wait until after sub-freezing temperatures occur to begin spring digging.

Fall planting is often done on the assumption that it permits a longer growing period for the new root system to become more established before the next hot, dry summer season, but research reports are conflicting. In some studies, fall planting did increase root and top growth by the end of the first growing season after planting (71,74,82). In other studies with different species (75,77) trees regenerated more new roots when planted in spring. Species differences or exact planting date could account for this conflicting information, but it does point out the need for additional research on a variety of species. We need to know more about how root regeneration is controlled throughout the seasons by factors such as hormones, carbohydrate supply, soil moisture, and temperature.

To take greatest advantage of fall planting in temperate climates, planting should be completed sufficiently early for roots to regenerate and support the plant during the winter. The soils must be warm long enough to permit new root growth to develop an adequate absorbing surface. According to one report, there should be at least four weeks between planting time and when the soil temperature drops to 40°F (4°C) (73).

Several weeks of 60°-70°F (15°-21°C) soil temperatures at the 6-12 in (15-30 cm) soil depth is especially important for root development of evergreens planted in the fall. Evergreens can loose considerable water through their leaves during fall and winter months. New root growth must be sufficiently developed, because if water loss greatly exceeds the rate of absorption, the needles or leaves will dehydrate and die. When evergreens are planted in the fall, it is imperative that the soil contains an ample supply of water before the soil freezes. Protection from desiccation with windscreens and anti-desiccants through the winter may also be required.

Planting on sites in temperate climates exposed to excessive wind should be delayed until spring, if possible. If fall planting is necessary in such sites, it must be done early enough to assure that new roots will develop before freezing weather. Evergreens should be shielded from prevailing winds by using burlap or other suitable wind barriers. Film antitranspirants have also proven beneficial.

In urban settings, intense heat reflected off of buildings, sidewalks, and streets causes prolonged high temperatures not encountered in rural or wooded areas. Prolonged periods of drought and drying winds, regardless of setting, cause frequent and severe water stress during summer. Fall planting may allow for additional root growth prior to the onset of these conditions and result in less stress.

TYPE OF STOCK AND PLANTING METHODS

It is possible to plant some species at virtually any time of the year if choices of nursery stock and planting methods are correct. Plants grown in containers can be planted successfully in any season because root loss is minimal. Bare root planting must be completed while the plant is dormant for a good chance of success. Field-grown plants and those in in-ground fabric bags are also best moved while plants are dormant. When moved while in the dormant state, the plant can adjust to the limited water supply from the reduced root system by producing smaller leaves in spring (76). Root loss while leaves are present causes the most stress because the fully developed crown will require more water. Drought stress can kill plants if transpiration exceeds the limited absorptive capacity of the root system, even if soil moisture is adequate. Though, field grown stock is best dug when dormant, some species can be dug in any season with proper care during and after transplanting (81). Summer transplanting may be more difficult in arid climates. Plants dug in-leaf from the nursery, and then stored for at least a few days in a protected holding area, are said to be "hardened-off." In the holding area, the process of root regeneration may be initiated, and the plant may also drop a few leaves, reducing transpiration. Therefore, the plant may be able to establish more quickly once moved to the more stressful landscape site. A hardening-off period often helps improve transplanting success (72).

Transplanting with tree spades may be more successful in the summer than balled and burlapped because the root ball can often be oversized without additional cost. Also, fine roots may be less disturbed when the root ball is supported by rigid blades during the entire process.

Some tree species can be transplanted in winter when the soil ball is frozen (Figure 4-1). The advantages of transplanting trees with frozen soil balls are primarily economical and mechanical. Contractors can extend the planting season and keep crews busy during the winter months. Large soil balls can be easier to handle and transport frozen, with less chance that the ball will crack and damage the roots. Soil balls with high sand or gravel content can be moved with less support while frozen. Frozen ground provides better access for heavy equipment at both the digging and the planting site.

Sugar maple (*Acer saccharum*), pine (*Pinus* sp.), honeylocust (*Gleditsia triacanthos*), elm (*Ulmus* sp.), linden (*Tilia* sp.), and crabapple (*Malus* sp.) are species most suited for winter transplanting. Red oak (*Quercus rubra*), dogwood (*Cornus florida*), hemlock (*Tsuga canadensis*), sycamore (*Platanus occidentalis*), sweetgum (*Liquidambar styraciflua*), birch (*Betula* sp.), and magnolia (*Magnolia* sp.) are less likely to survive.

Plants that are well suited for the planting site and carefully maintained after planting will have the widest latitude in planting dates. Substituting a different species or choosing a different type of nursery stock can also extend the planting season. It is possible to "beat the odds" on a few plants that are planted out of season in a small home garden if they receive special attention before and after planting. Larger landscapes where plants receive less individual attention are most successfully planted at the optimum time of year.

FIGURE 4-1. Frozen soil balls are easier to handle and transport with less chance that the ball will crack and damage the roots. Careful handling of the soil ball is essential. (photo credit - K. Bachtel)

LITERATURE CITED

70. Anisko, T. and O.M. Lindstrom. 1996. *Cold hardiness of evergreen azaleas is increased by water stress imposed at three dates.* J. Am. Soc. Hort. Sci. 121:296-300.

71. Dickinson, S. and C.E. Whitcomb. 1981. *Why nurserymen should consider fall transplanting.* Am. Nurseryman 153(10):11, 64-67.

72. Gilman, E.F. 1993. Establishing trees in the landscape pp. 69-77 **In** Watson, G.W. and D. Neely (Eds.), The Landscape Below Ground. International Society of Arboriculture, Savoy, IL. 222 pp.

73. Good, G.L. and T.E. Corell. 1982. *Field trials indicate the benefits and limits of fall planting.* Am. Nurseryman 156(8):31-34.

74. Harris, J.R., P. Knight, and J. Fanelli. 1996. *Fall transplanting improves establishment of balled and burlapped fringe tree* (Chionanthus virginicus L.). HortSci. 31:1143-1145.

75. Kelly, R.J. and B.C. Moser. 1983. *Root regeneration of* Liriodendron tulipifera *in response to auxin, stem pruning and environmental conditions.* J. Amer. Soc. Hort. Sci. 108:1085-1090.

76. Kjelgren, R., B. Cleveland, and M. Foutch. 1994. *Establishment of white oak seedling with three post-plant handling methods on deep tilled minesoil during reclamation.* J. Environ. Hort. 12:100-103.

77. Larson, M.M. 1984. *Seasonal planting, root regeneration and water deficits of Austrian pine and arborvitae.* J. Environ. Hort. 2:33-38.
78. Lathrop, J.K. and R.A. Mecklenburg. 1971. *Root regeneration and root dormancy in* Taxus *spp.* J. Amer. Soc. Hort. Sci. 96:111-114.
79. Pellett, H. 1980. *Relationship of fall watering practice to winter injury of conifers.* New Horizons. pp. 12-15.
80. Stone, E.C. and J.L. Jenkinson. 1970. *Influence of soil water on root growth capacity of ponderosa pine transplants.* For. Sci. 16:230-239.
81. Watson, G.W. and E.B. Himelick. 1982. *Seasonal variation in root regeneration of transplanted trees.* J. Arboric. 8:305-310.
82. Witherspoon, W.R. and G.P. Lumis. 1986. *Root regeneration, starch content, and root promoting activity in* T. cordata *cultivars at three different digging-planting times.* J. Environ. Hort. 4:76-79.

chapter

5

Obtaining Quality Plants

Proper plant selection and good site preparation must be followed by obtaining quality plants. The method used to produce a plant in the nursery can affect its survival in the landscape. Choosing the best nursery production method for each situation is essential. Amount of root loss, soil type, seasonal availability, and handling procedures vary with each type of stock.

Each production method has certain advantages and disadvantages. No single nursery production method fulfills the needs of every planting job. Methods that are practical, economical, and allow for planting throughout the year are the most widely used. Less versatile methods may be very well-suited for special situations. Understanding how each production method affects plants after they are installed in the landscape can help in selecting the best type of nursery stock for each situation.

ORIGIN OF PLANT MATERIAL

It is important to know the source of the plants you purchase. If plants were grown in local nurseries for several years, then they are likely to be tolerant of the local climate. Plants produced in nurseries from other regions with the same climate extremes can also be a safe choice. Plants shipped from nurseries in another region with a different climate may not be hardy unless the source of the plants used for propagation was from a region similar to yours and the plants possess the natural ability to withstand the climate extremes in your region.

Very little information may be available to the buyer on the source of rootstock used for grafted plants. Quality growers are usually aware of graft incompatibilities and may also be very careful to use rootstock that is hardy. Sources of seed for root stock may vary from grower to grower. Some may be very careful to obtain seed from northern parts of the species range to assure winter hardiness. Others may use convenient seed sources from nearby or from areas where seed of the species is plentiful and easy to collect. Seedlings with rapid, aboveground growth rates are most useful for grafting. These seed sources may have low root/shoot ratios (97,103) and may not be the best choice for producing a vigorous root system. Growers that are conscious of the need for a vigorous root system will often seek sources of seed with more vigorous root growth, though sources with the **most** vigorous root growth may still be passed over if shoot growth is not adequate.

How a grower produces and handles plants is also important. In an evaluation of similar plants shipped from 12 different nurseries, great variation was found in root development, tissue moisture content, and growth after planting (116). This variation could be due to differences in plant genetics, cultural practices or shipping conditions.

BARE ROOT PRODUCTION

Uses

The traditional bare root method of transplanting trees and shrubs continues to be popular in certain situations. Small bare root plants are available at garden centers, by mail order, and at local plant sales. Small seedlings are often distributed through Arbor Day and community tree planting programs. Some municipal tree planting programs plant up to 2 in (5 cm) bare root stock. Bare root stock is not commonly used by landscape contractors in the United States and Canada, but it may be more popular in Europe (112).

Limitations

This method is usually limited to small planting stock, but even large, mature deciduous trees have been transplanted bare root under optimum circumstances. Evergreens are seldom moved bare root. Difficulty digging out the root system and keeping it from drying out increases with size of the plant. For the best chance of success, dormant bare root plants should be planted in late winter or early spring to allow sufficient time for fine root development before the leaves emerge. Survival rates of small bare root plants will usually exceed that of large bare root plants (111).

Delayed planting of dormant stock often results in rapid bud break from exposure to warm air temperatures before sufficient fine root proliferation has occurred. Bare root plantings will usually be more successful in areas with moderate summer temperatures. In warmer climates where the dormant period is short, or does not occur at all, bare root planting can be difficult. Contractors who must plant all season cannot usually use bare root plants. In an analysis of one municipal tree planting program, bare root survival was so low that for the cost of one surviving bare root tree, two trees could be planted successfully with a tree spade (99). Though planting bare root has substantial limitations, success rates can be high if growing conditions and care after planting are favorable.

Description

Seedlings are usually grown in prepared beds with special soils. Introduction of ectomycorrhizal fungi can improve the growth of seedlings in completely sterilized nursery bed soils (101,118). Beds prepared with less extreme treatments do not require inoculation. Seedlings with taproots may be undercut (root pruned) to promote lateral root formation. Plants are usually grown in sandy or loamy field soils to facilitate bare root harvesting.

Variations

Process-balled plants are dug bare root, and then soil is added around roots to form a root ball. Biodegradable containers or burlap and twine are often used to provide support to the root ball soil. Since new roots can begin to proliferate in the soil ball, plants can be held for many weeks before planting. Shipping plants bare root from the nursery reduces cost, while creating a soil ball after shipping can extend the planting season if the plants are properly stored and maintained. Process-balled plants are most commonly encountered in retail outlets.

Selection

Root systems of bare root plants can only be evaluated after the plants have been dug. When purchasing plants from a local supplier, select plants from stock in overwinter storage, or visit the growing fields and ask the grower to dig a few random plants for you to examine. If you must order plants without being able to examine the root systems, use a supplier known for quality plants, and inspect the root systems after receiving them. Be sure your specifications are clear, and that the supplier understands you will reserve the right to reject a shipment of unacceptable plants.

When selecting bare root trees, consider the vigor and structure of the root system. A simple iodine stain test (139) can be performed on a few random woody roots to confirm the presence of adequately stored carbohydrates that will be needed for new root growth. Root spread should be adequate. Table 5-1 describes the relationship between caliper, height, and root spread. Another guideline sometimes used is that the root spread should equal four times the trunk circumference. Lateral root development is an important factor. Plants with strong taproots and little lateral root development will probably not survive transplanting well. Seedlings with at least four permanent first-order lateral roots (main roots coming from the base of the trunk, or the taproot) grow much better after transplanting than those with fewer lateral roots (106,118,125). Discarding plants with inferior root structure after receiving the shipment could result in additional expense, but the investment may be worth it. Also avoid plants if the root systems appear to be too dry.

TABLE 5-1. Examples of recommended minimum root spread for nursery grown bare root plants (84).

Caliper*		Height		Minimum Root Spread	
inches	cm	ft	m	inches	cm
Deciduous Shrubs					
—	—	2	0.6	11	28
—	—	3	0.9	14	35
—	—	4	1.2	16	40
—	—	5	1.5	18	45
—	—	6	1.8	20	50
Deciduous Trees					
½	1.25	5-6	1.5-1.8	12	30
1	2.5	8-10	2.4-3.0	18	45
1½	3.8	10-12	3.0-3.6	22	55
2	5.0	12-14	3.6-4.2	28	70

*Measured 4 in (10 cm) above ground level.

FIELD-GROWN WITH A SOIL BALL

Uses

This method, often referred to as balled and burlapped (B&B), may be the most common method of moving landscape sized plants in colder climates (i.e., hardiness zones 2-6). Plants dug in the dormant season can be held for planting throughout the season, though immediate planting is always best. Undisturbed fine root contact with the soil is a major factor in the success and versatility of this method. Contractors and municipalities use B&B stock frequently. The heavy root balls may limit homeowners to planting only small B&B trees and shrubs.

Limitations

B&B plants are usually dug while they are dormant in early spring or late fall to minimize post-planting stress. However, plants can sometimes be successfully moved in summer if given the proper care (140). Root pruning may increase survival rates of summer transplants. The heavy root balls can be expensive to transport and can limit the distance of distribution from the nursery.

Description

Trees are usually planted into nursery fields as whips that are often obtained from another nursery specializing in propagation. It is not uncommon for grafted trees to be planted with the roots too deep (93,122). Sometimes this is done intentionally so that the graft is below ground level in the nursery. This reduces sprouting from the root stock (Figure 5-1), and protects the graft area from her-bicides. When trees are planted with the graft below the soil, the roots are 2-4 in (5-10 cm) too deep and may therefore be too deep in the root ball when harvested (Figure 5-2). Cultivation practices that cause soil to accumulate near the base of the trunk can add to this problem (93). Sometimes mounding soil around the base of the trunk is deliberate in order to create an area of drier soil around the base of the plant where weeds will not readily germinate. Though these trees can grow well enough in the high quality soil of the nursery, they may struggle to survive when planted on difficult urban sites with heavy soils and poor drainage (137).

Variations

If done correctly, **root pruning** can result in a more branched and dense root system in the nursery (Figure 5-3). Some European nursery catalogs describe trees by size and number of times they have been root pruned or transplanted. Root pruning may be essential on wild-collected trees, due to the less dense and more spreading nature of their root systems. Because root pruning results in a substantial loss of roots, top growth is usually slowed and plants will take longer to reach marketable size. Some growers take advantage of slower growth after

FIGURE 5-1.   To prevent this type of sprouting from the understock, whips are often planted so that the graft is below the soil. The root system will then be too deep.

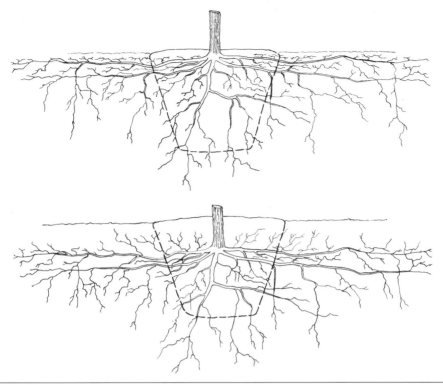

FIGURE 5-2. If the root system is too deep in the nursery, the root system may be confined to the bottom portion of the root ball.

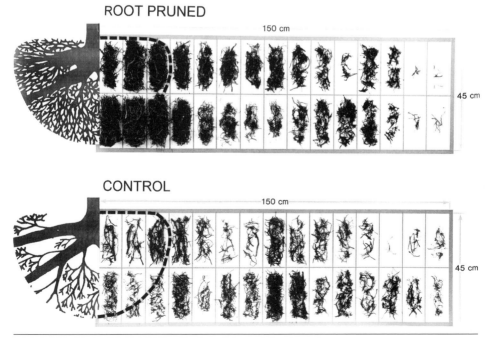

FIGURE 5-3. Correct root pruning procedures can increase the density of roots in the root ball substantially, but root loss is still very high (141).

moderate root pruning to produce plants with a more compact form. Roots must be pruned several inches closer to the trunk than where the edge of the root ball will be located when the tree is eventually harvested. If the root ball edge is located at the same place where the roots were pruned, all of the regenerated roots resulting from root pruning will be cut off, and the benefits of root pruning will be lost (112,141). Root pruning should take place early enough so that there is time for vigor to recover to normal levels before digging, but not so early that the regenerated roots have once again spread widely by the time the tree is harvested. In some situations **trickle irrigation** alone may promote a dense root system with limited spread if surrounding soils remain dry or otherwise less conducive to root growth (105,127).

In-ground fabric bags, or root control bags, are used to restrict root spread for greater ease in harvesting and to reduce the size of the root ball for economy in shipping (Figure 5-4). Plant size should be within specified limits for the size of the fabric bag (Table 5-2). Plants grown too long in the bags may become root bound and stunted.

The non-woven fabric sides of the bag are designed to constrict roots that penetrate the fabric, creating a dense proliferation of roots within the bag. The numerous small roots near the edge of the root ball may facilitate regeneration of new roots more quickly after planting (129,138,143). The bag must be removed before planting.

FIGURE 5-4. In-ground fabric bags are a system in which plants are grown in the field within specially designed fabric bags. The bags are intended to limit root growth outside of the bag and to develop a more branched root system in a smaller root ball, but research data have not always been supportive.

TABLE 5-2.   Examples of recommended minimum fabric bag sizes for nursery grown plants (84).

Caliper*		Height**		Fabric Bag Diameter	
inches	cm	ft	m	inches	cm
1½	3.8	4	1.2	12	30
2	5.0	6	1.8	16	40
2½	6.3	7	2.1	18	45
3	7.6	8	2.4	20	50
3½	8.9	10	3.0	22	55
4	10.2	12	3.7	24	60

*Deciduous trees measured 4 in (10 cm) above ground level.

**Shrubs and evergreens.

Results of research studies have been mixed on how well the bags actually perform in use (96,98,104,110,114,117). Species variation seems to be a major factor. Bags can be difficult to remove if many roots are protruding through the fabric after it is dug. Newer in-ground fabric bag designs have helped overcome this problem (87). Trickle irrigation may be necessary in both the nursery and the landscape after planting to avoid drought stress from the restricted root system and small root ball (108,129).

Balled and potted plants are those that are dug with a ball of earth and placed into a container instead of being wrapped with burlap. This method allows plants to be sold throughout the season, providing the flexibility of root balls without the precise digging and wrapping involved with balling and burlapping. In climates without extremely cold winter temperatures, nurseries can keep plants in these aboveground containers for more than one season, enlarging the diameter and pruning the roots periodically (Figure 5-5). Field soils will have different drainage characteristics in containers with bottoms and may become poorly drained. This method should only be used with well-drained soils.

Plants collected from other landscapes or wild lands usually have root systems that are less dense and more spreading than nursery grown plants. Consequently, the standards (84) call for the root ball to be increased to the next largest size class of plant.

Selection

Plants should be selected and tagged at the nursery if possible. Plants selected should be specially marked so that species and cultivars can later be identified. Often it is best to mark the trunk on the north side for later orientation in the planting process. Select trees with several major lateral roots at, or just below, the soil surface. These are often the most vigorous trees in the row.

On trees over 2 in (5 cm) caliper, a pronounced root flare may have started to develop, indicating strong formation of lateral roots. On smaller trees, use a

FIGURE 5-5. A type of balled and potted system. If the plants are held in the container for more than one season, the diameter of these containers can be enlarged. Sometimes the container wall is replaced with burlap and wire cloth for shipping.

simple test. Grasp the trunk about 4 ft (1.2 m) above the ground and gently move it in a circular or rocking motion. If the first roots are too deep, the trunk will pivot deep in the soil, and a small gap will form between the trunk and the surrounding soil. A space around the trunk may have already opened from natural trunk movement in the wind. If the tree is planted at the proper depth, the trunk will pivot at or just below the surface, and no space will develop around it (Figure 5-6). When the plants are delivered, be sure the root ball diameter and depth (Table 5-3 and 5-4) are appropriate for the size of the plant, and that the soil is firm, indicating adequate roots in the ball.

CONTAINER PRODUCTION

Container production is the most rapidly growing segment of the nursery industry. Many of the reasons for its rapid growth are related to business and logistic considerations. In container production, nursery site selection is less soil type dependent than field production because specially prepared media are used in the containers. Containers can be rearranged for efficient use of space. Lightweight, soil-less media can be less expensive to ship and easier to handle at the planting site.

Uses

In warmer regions (i.e., hardiness zones 7-11), container production is a common method of nursery production. Even large trees are container-grown in climates

FIGURE 5-6.   A space will open at the base of the trunk from wind movement when the root system of a small tree is too deep (left), compared to a tree planted at the proper depth (right).

where overwintering is not a concern. Containers can be as large as 500 gal (2000 l). The largest containers are often boxes constructed of wood. Since few roots are lost in the planting process, plants can be available from the nursery throughout the year.

Limitations

In the north, cold, root-killing temperatures in the container media can limit the use of containers in nurseries to smaller plants which can be covered over the winter. Larger container plants sold in these regions are generally shipped from warmer climates.

High soil temperatures (112-122°F, 45-50°C) on the sun exposed side of the pot can be a concern (94,102,113,115,121,144). Heat stress on roots during production can cause an inhibition of root growth for up to 4 months after the plants are installed in the landscape (120,133).

Container soils must be well drained in order to provide sufficient aeration while in the pot. Once the container root ball is planted in the landscape, water moves easily from the coarse container soil to the finer textured landscape soil, and the root ball holds less water than it did in the container (Figure 5-7) (100,126,135). Irrigation may not be as frequent in the landscape as it was in the nursery, resulting in high levels of water stress even though there was minimal loss of roots (108). Frequent watering will be required for at least the first season, especially if planted in summer.

TABLE 5-3. Examples of recommended minimum size of soil ball for nursery grown plants (84).

Caliper*		Minumum Height**		Ball Diameter	
in	cm	ft	m	in	cm
—	—	1	0.3	8	20
—	—	2	0.6	10	25
½	1.25	3	0.9	12	30
¾	1.9	4	1.2	14	35
1	2.5	5	1.5	16	40
1½	3.8	7	2.1	20	50
2	5.0	9	2.7	24	60
2½	6.3	10	3.0	28	70
3	7.5	13	4.0	32	80
3½	8.9	17	5.1	38	96
4	10.2	—	—	42	107
5	12.7	—	—	54	137
6***	15.0	—	—	—	—

* Caliper of the trunk measured 6 in (15 cm) above the ground up to and including 4 in (10 cm) size, and 12 in (30 cm) above the ground for larger sizes.
** For small trees up to 5 ft (1.5 m), deciduous shrubs up to 9 ft (2.7 m), and columnar evergreens over 3 ft (0.9 m). Root balls of conical evergreens and broadleaf evergreens are at least one size larger.
***Trees 6 in (15 cm) and greater caliper should have a root ball of 10 in (25 cm) diameter per inch of trunk caliper, that is, a 7 in (18 cm) tree should have a 70 in (1.8 m) diameter root ball.

TABLE 5-4. Relationship between diameter and depth of the root ball (84).

Ball Diameter	Ball Depth
less than 20 in (50 cm)	75% of width
20-30 in (50-75 cm)	67% of width
31-40 in (76-100 cm)	60% of width & drum laced

Because the container restricts the spread of the root system, lateral roots reaching the sides often continue to grow around the inside of the pot and become circling roots (Figure 5-8). Circling roots can strangle the plant a few years after planting as both the roots and the stem grow larger, especially if they are located on the top half of the root ball. High soil temperatures from sun

FIGURE 5-7. Light container soil media is needed for good drainage in container production, but can become excessively well-drained once installed in the landscape.

exposure, or saturated soils in the bottom of the container from over irrigation, may help to eliminate circling roots but are not good management practices. Various pot designs with ridges and holes have been developed to prevent circling roots (85,86,128,142). Though the roots do not circle as much, many roots still grow against the inside of the container wall. A recently developed technique is to apply a coating containing copper hydroxide to the inside wall of the pot or to use a fabric liner impregnated with the same compound, in order to stunt the roots as they contact the inside of the container (Figure 5-10) (88,89,90,91,95,119,123,136). Root response to the copper treatment may or may not result in better root growth after planting (94,136). Not all species respond well to the copper treatments (92,136). In the correct concentration, the copper compound does not appear to be toxic to the plant (83,132).

Variations

Plants in aboveground containers are subject to being blown over, often resulting in substantial increases in maintenance expense. New in-ground container production systems reduce blow over and provide a more stable soil

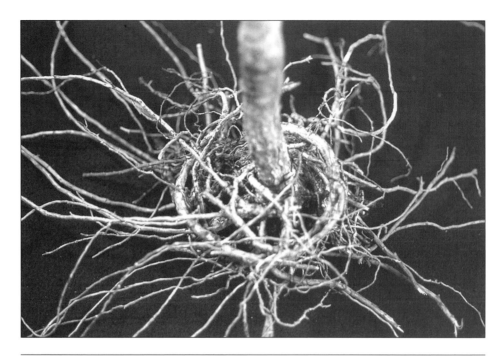

FIGURE 5-8.   Circling roots can develop inside containers and cause problems after planting.

FIGURE 5-9.   Containers designed to minimize circling roots may have ridges that deflect circling roots or openings that air prune roots. Roots may still grow extensively against the inside of the container wall, even though they don't circle.

FIGURE 5-10. The plant on the left was grown in a pot with a copper compound applied to the inside wall of the container to minimize circling roots and root growth against the container wall. The plant on the right was grown in an untreated container. (photo credit— B. Appleton)

temperature. Soils in pot-in-pot containers can be 29°F (16°C) cooler in summer (133,134). Since the plants are grown on wider spacings than typical containers, crowns are larger and trunk taper is improved. Pot-in-pot systems (86,109,130,131) involve sinking an outer pot (socket or holder) into the ground, and inserting a second pot (the actual pot that is harvested with the plant) in the pot that is buried in the ground (Figure 5-11). Roots growing between the pots are lost when harvested. This can make moving them in summer more stressful than traditional container systems.

Low profile containers are wider than conventional containers (30 in, 76 cm) and allow for more natural lateral root development. Circling roots are less likely to develop. Low profile containers resist blow over during production and after planting (Figure 5-12) (124). The shallow wide root ball of low profile containers may be an advantage when planted on poorly drained sites. Traditional taller container designs may be best for landscape sites where the most consistent soil moisture is found in deeper soils.

Selection

Root systems of container-grown plants should be well developed and hold the soil ball together when it is removed from the container. Avoid plants that are pot-bound or have circling roots. Multiple layers of circling roots that develop within the root ball from successive stages of production can be difficult to detect (Figure 5-13). Plants should be the appropriate size for their container (84) (Table 5-5).

FIGURE 5-11. Pot-in-pot container production systems make the plants more stable and less susceptible to cold winter soil temperatures. (photo credit—B. Appleton)

FIGURE 5-12. Low profile containers are more suited to the spreading nature of root systems. (photo credit—B. Appleton)

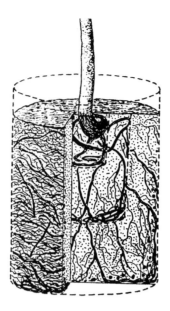

FIGURE 5-13. Multiple layers of circling roots can develop from successive stages of production. (Drawing courtesy of R.W. Harris. Arboriculture: Integrated Management of Landscape Trees, Shrubs and Vines. 2nd ed. © 1992, p. 74. Reprinted by permission of Prentice Hall, Englewood Cliffs, NJ.)

TABLE 5-5. Examples of recommended minimum container sizes for nursery grown plants (84).

Caliper*		Height**			Container size	
inches	cm	feet	meters	#	gallons	liters
—	—	1	0.3	—	0.7-1.1	2.5-4.1
—	—	2	0.6	1	0.7-1.1	2.5-4.1
—	—	3	0.9	1	0.7-1.1	2.5-4.1
—	—	4	1.2	2	1.4-2.0	5.2-7.8
—	—	5	1.5	4	3.4-4.2	12.9-16.0
—	—	6	1.8	5	4.7-5.4	16.5-20.4
1	2.5	7	2.1	7	5.8-7.8	21.9-29.3
—	—	8	2.4	10	9.0-11.5	34.1-43.4
1½	3.8	—	—	15	12.0-16.0	45.4-60.6
2	5.0	—	—	25	25.0-29.7	94.6-112.4
2½	6.3	—	—	25	25.0-29.7	94.6-112.4

*Deciduous trees measured 4 in (10 cm) above ground level.

**Only deciduous shrubs included in table. Evergreens are measured by height, but container size depends on both size and shape, and are generally 1 to 2 sizes larger than for deciduous plants.

PLANT QUALITY

Plants produced by all nursery methods should meet certain basic quality standards. Only healthy plants with well-formed tops that are characteristic of the species should be planted. The proper relationship between caliper and height for trees and shrubs is well described in the American Standard for Nursery Stock (84). Heights greater than those listed for a given caliper indicate a spindly trunk that may not be capable of standing upright without support when in full leaf. A tapered trunk decreases in diameter with height. On small caliper trees, rigidly staking a tree prevents trunk flexing and results in a tall, spindly, poorly tapered trunk. A staking system that allows some side-to-side movement of the trunk encourages taper development.

Proper distribution of branches also promotes development of good trunk taper. For best trunk development, one half of the foliage should be growing on branches that originate along the lower two-thirds of the trunk (107). Trees grown for street plantings and other landscape uses where pedestrian and vehicle traffic are expected nearby must often be pruned up higher.

Branches on broad-leaved trees should be well spaced, both vertically and around the circumference, for strong attachments and unrestricted flow of water and nutrients in the trunk. The practice of heading back the leader to encourage lateral branches can lead to several branches originating at the same point. This can result in a very weak structure that is susceptible to storm damage as the tree grows (Figure 5-14). If still present when purchased, it is very important to prune

FIGURE 5-14.   The practice of heading back trees in the nursery to stimulate branching can result in an undesirable group of branches originating at the same point. If excess branches have not been removed at the nursery, prune them out at planting time.

out some of these branches, leaving those with the best position and branch attachment (see Chapter 7). The central leader should be reestablished in the nursery. Conifers normally form numerous branches (whorl) at the same level with each year's growth.

Branches should diverge from the trunk at a wide angle except in cultivars that normally grow in narrow, upright (fastigiate) forms. Trees with included bark in the branch crotches should be avoided (Figure 5-15). Pruning wounds on the trunk should not exceed 1 in (2.5 cm) diameter or 25 percent of the circumference of the trunk, which ever is smaller, and should be completely closed. Good nursery practices include pruning to develop good branch structure early in production. Large pruning cuts or little callus formation indicate that pruning was delayed too long. The base of the trunk should be examined for evidence of girdling roots, mechanical injury, and gnawing injury by rodents.

On grafted trees, abnormal growth differences at the union can indicate a problem. Weak graft unions can break in heavy winds, even years after planting. Substantial differences in bark characteristics above and below the graft usually indicate that the rootstock is not the same species as the scion. This is often acceptable, but know the origin of the rootstock to be certain that the roots will be adapted to the planting site. Certain species are very prone to producing basal sprouts from the rootstock. If the scion dies during an early stage of production, it is possible for a sprout from the rootstock to replace it without being noticed. Be sure that the tree is true to cultivar name.

Trees should exhibit adequate twig growth during the most recent 2 to 4 years and have well-formed buds (Figure 5-16). Normal twig growth may vary from

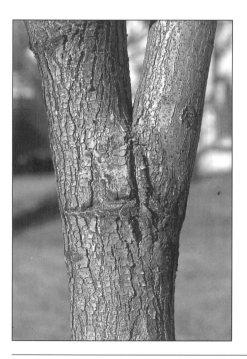

FIGURE 5-15. Trees with included bark in crotches (left) should be avoided. The bark should push up to form a small ridge in the crotch (right).

4 to 48 in (10 to 120 cm) annually and should be characteristic of the species. Trees and shrubs should be vigorous specimens free from insects and diseases. Trunk bark should be firm, with no indication of fungus cankers or galls, insect borers, dieback, frost cracks, sunscald, or mechanical injury.

Palms that have been subjected to long-term stresses caused by severe nutritional or water deficiencies often display a constriction of the trunk that corresponds to the period of time during which the stress occurred (Figure 5-17). The

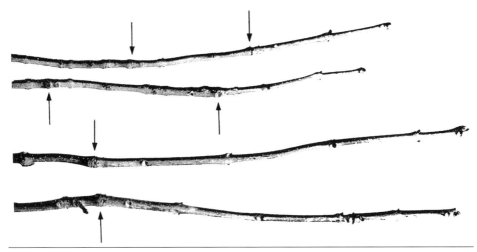

FIGURE 5-16. Comparison of twig growth and bud development. The lower two twigs are from a vigorous white ash tree. The current season growth between the tips and the bud scale scars, indicated by arrows, is long and thick and has plump buds. The upper two twigs, from a less vigorous tree, indicates shorter annual growth and have smaller buds and more spindly twigs.

FIGURE 5-17. Constriction of a palm trunk is caused by long-term stress. Avoid these plants.

constrictions inhibit the translocation of water and nutrients in the vascular system. Such trees are also less able to withstand wind damage. Only specimens that have not developed severe constrictions of the trunk area should be selected. In addition, palm species that exhibit severe symptoms of nutritional deficiency, usually caused by inadequate manganese, should not be selected.

To obtain the best plants possible, you must be sure that the source is compatible with your region, and this includes the rootstock. The nursery production method must be right for the time and place you are planting. And of course, the vigor and health of the plants must be excellent. Choosing high quality plants, along with choosing the right plant and proper site preparation all contribute to planting success.

LITERATURE CITED

83. Aldrich, J. H., J.G. Norcini, and W.E. Roddenberry, Jr. 1996. *Effect of cupric hydroxide-treated containers on bougainvillea propagation and growth after transplanting.* J. Environ. Hort. 14:181-183.

84. Anonymous, 1996. American Standard For Nursery Stock. American Association of Nurserymen, Washington, D.C. 57 pp.

85. Appleton, B.L. 1989. *Evaluation of nursery container designs for minimization or prevention of root circling.* J. Environ. Hort. 7:79-61.

86. Appleton, B.L. 1993. *Nursery production alternatives for reduction or elimination of circling tree roots.* J. Arboric. 19:383-388.

87. Appleton, B.L. 1995. *Nursery production methods for improving tree roots-An update.* J. Arboric. 21:265-270.

88. Arnold, M.A. 1992. *Timing, acclimation period, and cupric hydroxide concentration alter growth responses of the Ohio production system.* J. Environ. Hort. 10:114-117.

89. Arnold, M.A. and D.K. Struve. 1989. *Green ash establishment following transplant.* J. Amer. Soc. Hort. Sci. 114:591-595.

90. Arnold, M.A. and D.K. Struve. 1993. *Root distribution and mineral uptake of coarse-rooted trees grown in cupric hydroxide-treated containers.* HortSci. 28:988-992.

91. Arnold, M.A. and E. Young. 1991. $CuCO_3$-*painted containers and root pruning affect apple and green ash root growth and cytokinin levels.* HortSci. 26:242-244.

92. Beeson, R.C. and R. Newton. 1992. *Shoot and root responses of 18 southeastern woody landscape species grown in cupric hydroxide-treated containers.* J. Environ. Hort. 10:214-217.

93. Berrang, P., D.F. Karnosky, and B.J. Stanton. 1985. *Environmental factors affecting tree health in New York City.* J. Arboric. 11:185-189.

94. Brass, T.J., G.J. Keever, D.J. Eakes, and C.H. Gilman. 1996. *Styrene-lined and copper-coated containers affect production and landscape establishment of red maple.* HortSci. 3:353-356.

95. Burdett, A.N. and P.A.F. Martin. 1982. *Chemical root pruning of coniferous seedlings.* HortSci. 17:622-624.

96. Chong, C., G.P. Lumis, R.A. Cline, and H.J. Reissmann. 1987. *Growth and chemical composition of* Populus deltoides x nigra *grown in field-grow fabric containers.* J. Environ. Hort. 5:45-48.

97. Cock, J.H. 1982. *Cassava: a basic energy source in the tropics.* Science 218:755-762.

98. Cole, J.C. and D.L. Hensley. 1994. *Field-grow fabric containers do not affect transplant survival or establishment of green ash.* J. Arboric. 20:120-123.

99. Cool, R.A. 1976. *Tree spade vs. bare root planting.* J. Aboric. 2:92-95.

100. Costello, L. and J.L. Paul. 1975. *Moisture relations in transplanted container plants.* HortSci. 10:371-372.

101. Dixon, R.K. and P.S. Johnson. 1992. *Synthesis of ectomycorrhizae on Northern red oak seedlings in a Michigan nursery.* J. Aboric. 18:266-272.

102. Fretz, T.A. 1971. *Influence of physical conditions on summer temperatures in nursery containers.* HortSci. 6:400-401.

103. Geng, M.C. 1989. *A provenance test of white elm* Ulmus pumila *L. in China.* Silvae Genetica 38:37-44.

104. Gilman, E.F. 1992. *Effect of root pruning southern magnolia prior to transplanting on rate of establishment in the landscape.* HortSci. 18:197-200.

105. Gilman, E.F., G.W. Knox, C.A. Neal, and U. Yadav. 1994. *Microirrigation affects growth and root distribution of trees in fabric containers.* HortTech. 4:43-45.

106. Gossard, A.C. 1942. *Root and shoot production by young pecan trees treated with indole-butyric acid at the time of transplanting.* Proc. Am. Soc. Hort. Sci. 41:161-166.

107. Harris, R.W. 1992. Arboriculture: Integrated Management of Landscape Trees, Shrubs and Vines. Prentice Hall, Englewood Cliffs, NJ. 674 pp.

108. Harris, J.R. and E.F. Gilman. 1993. *Production method affects growth and post-transplant establishment of* East Palatka *holly.* J. Am. Soc. Hort. Sci. 118:194-200.

109. Harris, J.R., A.X. Niemiera, R.D. Wright, and C.H. Parkerson. 1996. *Chemically controlling root escape in pot-in-pot production of river birch and yoshino cherry.* HortTech. 6:30-34.

110. Hensley, D.L. 1993. *Harvest method has no influence on growth of transplanted green ash.* J. Arboric. 19:379-382.

111. Hodge, S.J. 1991. *Improving the growth of established amenity trees: Site physical conditions.* Arboric. Res. Note 102-91-ARB:1-4. Forestry Commission, U.K.

112. Hvass, N. 1994. *Roots.* Arborist News 3(6): 9-11.

113. Ingram, D.L. 1981. *Characterization of temperature fluctuations and woody plant growth in white poly bags and conventional black containers.* HortSci. 16:762-763.

114. Ingram, D.L., U. Yadav, and C.A. Neal. 1987. *Do fabric containers restrict root growth in the deep south?* Am. Nurseryman (Sept.): 91-96.

115. Keever, G.S. and G.S. Cobb. 1984. *Container and production bed mulch effects on media temperatures and growth of* Hersheys Red *Azalea.* HortSci. 19:439-441.

116. Kendle, A.D., P. Gilberston, and A.D. Bradshaw. 1988. *The influence of stock source on transplant.* J. Arboric. 12:257-272.

117. Kjelgren, R. 1994. *Growth and water relations of Kentucky coffee tree in protective shelters during establishment.* HortSci. 29:777-780.

118. Kormanik, P.P., R.C. Schultz, and W.C. Bryan. 1982. *The influence of vesicular-arbuscular mycorrhizae on the growth and development of eight hardwood species.* For. Sci. 28:531-539.

119. Martin, C.A. and S. Bhattacharya. 1995. *Effects of cupric hydroxide-treated containers on growth of four southwestern desert landscape trees.* J. Arboric. 21:235-238.

120. Martin, C.A. and D.L. Ingram. 1991. *Root growth of Southern magnolia following exposure to high root zone temperatures.* HortSci. 26:370-371.

121. Martin, C.A. and D.L. Ingram. 1993. *Container dimension affects rooting medium temperature patterns.* HortSci. 28:18-19.

122. McClure, S. 1991. *Fatal flaws (overlooking critical practices for planting B&B material may prove deadly)*. Am. Nurseryman 174(8): 58-61.

123. McDonald, S.E., R.W. Tinus, and C.P.P. Reid. 1984. *Modification of ponderosa pine root systems in containers*. J. Environ. Hort. 2:1-5.

124. Milbocker, D.C. 1991. *Low-profile containers for nursery-grown trees*. HortSci. 26:261-263.

125. Nambiar, E.K.S. 1980. *Root configuration and root regeneration in* Pinus radiata *seedlings*. N.Z. For. Sci. 10:249-63.

126. Nelms, L.R. and L.A. Spomer. 1983. *Water retention of container soils transplanted into ground beds*. HortSci. 18:863-866.

127. Ponder, H.G. and A.L. Kenworthy. 1976. *Trickle irrigation of shade trees growing in the nursery: II. Influence on root distribution*. J. Amer. Soc. Hort. Sci. 101:104-107.

128. Privett, D.W. and R.L. Hummel. 1992. *Root and shoot growth of 'Coral Beauty' cotoneaster and leyland cypress produced in porous and nonporous containers*. J. Environ. Hort. 10:133-136.

129. Reiger, R. and C. Whitcomb. 1985. *A root control system for growing and transplanting trees*. Arboricultural J. 9:33-38.

130. Roberts, D.R. 1993. *How pot-in-pot systems save time, money*. Nursery Manager 9(6): 46, 48, 50).

131. Ruter, J.M. 1993. *Growth and landscape performance of three landscape plants produced in conventional and pot-in-pot production systems*. J. Environ. Hort. 11:124-127.

132. Ruter, J.M. 1994. *Growth responses of four vigorous-rooted tree species in cupric hydroxide-treated containers*. HortSci. 29:1089.

133. Schluckebier, J.G. and C.A. Martin. 1997. *Effects of above-ground pot-in-pot (PIP) placement and humic acid extract on growth of crape myrtle*. J. Environ. Hort. 15(1): 41-44.

134. Schuch, U.K. and D.R. Pittenger. 1996. *Root and shoot growth of eucalyptus in response to container configuration and copper carbonate*. HortSci. 31:165.

135. Spomer, L.A. 1980. *Container soil water relations: Production, maintenance, and transplanting*. J. Arboric. 6:315-320.

136. Struve, D.K. 1993. *Effect of copper-treated containers on transplant survival and regrowth of four tree species*. J. Environ. Hort. 11:196-199.

137. Switzer, G.L. 1960. *Exposure and planting depth effects on loblolly pine planting stock on poorly drained sites*. J. Forestry 58:390-391.

138. van de Werken, H. 1982. *Effects of four root barrier fabrics on penetration and self pruning of roots*. SNA Res. Conf. pp. 292-293.

139. Wargo, P.M. 1975. Estimating starch content in roots of deciduous trees-A visual technique. USDA For. Serv. Res. Pap. NE-313 9 pp.

140. Watson, G.W. and E.B. Himelick. 1982. *Seasonal variation in root regeneration of transplanted trees*. J. Arboric. 8:305-310.

141. Watson, G.W., and T.D. Sydnor. 1987. *The effect of root pruning on the root system of nursery trees*. J. Arboric. 13:126-130.

142. Whitcomb, C.E. 1985. *Innovations and the nursery industry*. J. Environ. Hort. 3:33-38.

143. Whitcomb, C.E. 1987. Establishment and Maintenance of Landscape Plants. Lacebark Publications, Stillwater, OK. 618 pp.

144. Young K. and K.R.W. Hammett. 1980. *Temperature patterns in exposed black polyethylene plant containers*. Agr. Meteorol. 21:165-172.

Section III

The Planting Process

Digging is the first step in the planting process for field-grown plants. How plants are treated between the growing fields and the planting site can affect the quality of all plants. It is important to know what to look for and to be prepared to reject inferior stock when it is delivered to the site.

Planting is more than just covering the root ball with soil. Attention to detail can help assure rapid establishment and long life. Recent research is influencing practices such as site preparation, soil amendments, and even staking. Wires, ropes, and wraps that are installed at planting can all cause damage if not used properly and removed in a timely manner.

Some planting jobs require special procedures or extraordinary ingenuity. Palms are not woody plants and react differently to injuries. You may be surprised at the tremendous size of some trees that are transplanted. Only specially qualified professionals can accomplish this successfully, but you might be interested to know what is possible.

Landscape professionals and home gardeners alike should take the time to become familiar with the research behind tree and shrub planting, and do the job right the first time. It is very difficult to go back to correct mistakes.

chapter

6

Digging, Handling, and Storing Plants

The grower's job does not stop with producing quality plants in the growing fields. The grower is often responsible for assuring that the plants arrive at the job site or retail outlet in the same excellent condition they left the nursery. The grower digs the plants, stores them until they are shipped, and often arranges for the shipping. If care is not taken during these steps, quality plants ready for harvest may not be quality plants when received by the customer.

TYING BRANCHES

Tops of spreading or low-branching plants should be tied before digging to provide clearance and to avoid damage during harvest and shipping. Care should be taken to avoid injuring the bark and splitting or breaking branches. Limbs should not be tied so tightly that the bark is compressed by a sharp bend at the base of the branch. On taller trees, the branches can sometimes be tied after the tree has been dug and tipped.

BARE ROOT PLANTS

Root spread

Smaller deciduous trees and shrubs can be dug bareroot. The American Standard for Nursery Stock (146) lists minimum rootspread standards in relation to tree size. Table 5-1 is a summary of these specifications. Plants collected from native stands should be dug with a root spread one-third greater than the spread of roots listed in the table.

Digging procedures

Bare root nurseries usually have well drained soils because plants can be removed with less damage to the roots. In the nursery, deciduous trees and shrubs are dug in the fall as they go dormant. If deciduous plants are dug before reaching the dormant stage, they may grow very poorly when replanted. Mechanized harvesting equipment, often a tractor-drawn U-blade, is used for lifting the plants from nursery rows (Figure 6-1). Trimming the tops and roots may be required after harvest.

Small numbers of plants can be dug by hand, but soil must still be sandy or well aggregated to remove the soil from the roots without excessive damage. Plants in heavy clay soils may be very difficult to dig bare root without excessive damage to the roots.

To dig small plants harvested with a root spread of less than 16 in (40 cm) drive a sharp spade into the ground at a slight angle to a depth of 1 ft (30 cm) around the entire plant at, or beyond, the minimum root spread distance. Gently pry up the roots and soil. A second pass around the circle will cut any roots missed the first time, and finish breaking loose the soil beneath the plant. The plant should not be lifted until all of the roots have been severed. Occasionally the plant must

FIGURE 6-1. Bare root trees being harvested in the nursery. (photo credit - K. Warren)

be tipped so that vertical roots can be severed with a sharp spade or pruning shears. Shake the loose soil from the roots before lifting it from the hole.

For larger plants, most of the soil will have to be removed from the roots before the plant is moved. Dig a circular trench just beyond the limits of the root spread to be harvested. Using a narrow-tined spading fork or similar tool, gently work the soil loose from the roots starting at the trench and working towards the center until most of the roots are exposed. The soil that falls into the trench should be removed periodically. Near the end, tip the plant to cut vertical roots. Keep the exposed roots as moist as possible while digging by covering them and periodically spraying them with a fine mist of water.

Overwinter storage

Fall harvesting has advantages. Fields are not usually as wet in the fall, avoiding the possibility that wet spring weather could delay harvest. Fall dug plants can be available at the appropriate time, even if the plants are being shipped to an area with an earlier spring.

Plants are often heeled-in with sawdust or mulch for the winter (Figure 6-2). Buildings with controlled temperature and humidity are also used. Cold storage is necessary to meet the normal winter chilling requirements of the fall-harvested plants. Increased chilling duration enhances the rate of root regeneration of seedlings until the maximum requirements of each species are met (167). It then decreases if stored too long, possibly due to carbohydrate depletion (155,159). The optimum storage temperature appears to be just above freezing (152).

Sensitivity to desiccation stress during nursery handling is the main reason for poor root regrowth of bare root plants. Plants loose water from both roots and

FIGURE 6-2. Bare root stock harvested in the fall is often heeled-in over the winter until it is shipped for spring planting. The same technique can be used to store plants on the job site. (photo credit - K. Warren)

stems while in cold storage (148). Plants harvested in complete dormancy are more resistant to desiccation during storage than plants harvested in early stages of dormancy (151,156,160).

Heeling-in

When storing a limited number of plants at the job site for a short period, plants should be heeled-in by covering the roots and lower portion of the stems with moist soil or mulch. Small evergreens should not be heeled-in because of damage to the closely packed tops. The plants should be shaded to keep the tops cool. **Plant before the buds break. Do not attempt to overwinter plants in cold climates while heeled-in.**

Shipping

Conditions during shipping are as important as during storage. Covered, temperature-controlled trucks should be used for long distance transport. Roots must be packed in moist peat moss, straw, sawdust, or wood chips

PLANTS WITH A SOIL BALL

Ball size

Larger sizes of deciduous trees and shrubs, and all but the smallest evergreens, are dug with a soil ball. Nursery grown stock can be dug by hand or with mechanical devices especially designed for nursery conditions. The ball size depends upon such factors as the size and species of plant and the type of soil in which it is growing. Table 5-3 lists recommended minimum root ball sizes in the United States for trees with well-branched root systems, grown in the nursery under favorable conditions, and receiving average care after planting. The standards in England are similar (145). Official standards in other countries may vary or may not be published. Some growers increase these minimum sizes significantly based on their experience. Species that are normally difficult to transplant (Table 2-3) should have larger soil balls than those of species that are easily moved. Trees collected from native stands should be dug with a root ball at least one size larger than listed in Table 5-3.

Soils balls are heavy. Table 6-1 lists approximate weights. A mass of soil without roots should be avoided. Heavy clay on the bottom of a ball adds considerable weight and contains few roots. If the root ball is dug shallower than normal for this reason, add extra width to make-up for the missing roots. The physical properties of many soils, however, require a greater depth to insure that the soil ball will not fracture during transport to the new site.

Digging and shaping the ball

In temperate climates, plants with soil balls are generally dug when they are dormant. Summer digging requires special hardening-off procedures discussed later in this chapter. Trees that will be transplanted during winter should be

TABLE 6-1. Estimated weight of soil balls.

Ball Diameter		Ball Depth		Approximate Ball and Tree Weight			
in	cm	in	cm	lbs	kg	US tons	Metric tons
10	25	8	20	34	15	—	—
12	30	9	23	55	25	—	—
14	35	11	28	91	42	—	—
16	40	12	30	124	56	—	—
18	45	14	35	193	88	—	—
20	50	15	38	254	115	—	—
24	60	16	41	392	178	—	—
28	70	19	48	624	283	—	—
32	80	20	50	867	394	—	—
36	90	22	55	1216	552	—	—
42	105	25	63	1877	853	—	—
48	120	29	74	—	—	1.5	1.3
60	150	32	81	—	—	2.4	2.2
72	180	34	86	—	—	3.7	3.4
84	210	36	91	—	—	5.4	4.9
96	240	38	96	—	—	7.4	6.8
108	280	40	100	—	—	9.9	9.0
120	300	40	100	—	—	12.2	11.1

selected in the fall and mulched with straw or wood chips before the ground freezes.

Small plants are most often dug by hand, as are small numbers of larger trees. Growers digging large numbers of plants during the busy and short harvest seasons use mechanical diggers (a type of tree spade) for greater efficiency (Figure 6-3). Trenching machines and backhoes are sometimes used to rough-dig very large trees before shaping the soil ball by hand.

Hand digging procedures vary somewhat by size of the root ball. Digging, wrapping, and handling root balls correctly takes skill, experience, and specialized equipment. If not done correctly, the root ball will break apart, roots will be damaged, and the plant may not survive. Inexperienced individuals should attempt only small root balls.

If the soil is dry, it should be moistened 2-3 days prior to digging. The plant will be less stressed if well watered. The soil will be easier to dig and will hold together better when moist. If the soil is excessively wet, the root ball will not be stable enough to hold its shape (Figure 6-4), and damage to fine roots will result.

Sod or loose soil should be carefully removed from around the plant. The first major roots should be within 1 in (2.5 cm) of the root ball surface. If the roots are too deep, and an excessive amount of surface soil has to be removed before starting the root ball, digging the root ball may be very difficult. Avoid this type of plant.

FIGURE 6-3. Growers use mechanical root ball digging machinery. Many have tires or tracks that allow access to wet fields in the spring.

FIGURE 6-4. When root balls are too wet, or if they lack adequate roots, they can be easily distorted during handling and transport, causing damage to many fine roots.

Mark the size of the desired root ball. About 4 in (10 cm) beyond the perimeter of the root ball, drive a sharp spade into the ground at least 12 in (30 cm) all the way around the plant, cutting as many small and medium size roots as possible. Dig a trench on the outside of the circular spade cut to at least three-quarters of the depth of the root ball.

With the back of the spade toward the plant, shave off enough soil to reduce the root ball to its final diameter, with a rounded top edge and uniformly tapered sides. Smaller balls should be nearly oval in profile. Larger root balls should be 6-12 in (15-30 cm) smaller at the base than at the widest point just below the rounded top edge. One side of a large root ball may be flattened if it will be transported on a trailer bed in the horizontal position.

All roots should be cut flush with the face of the root ball. Sharp hand shears or loppers should be used to cut large roots. If a spade is used for cutting large roots, it will jar the roots and loosen the ball. A clean sharp cut reduces split and torn roots, and results in less dieback.

Winter digging

A few extra precautions are required for when plants are moved with frozen soil balls. Although the term frozen soil ball is commonly used, in reality, only the outer 4-6 in (10-15 cm) of the ball soil should be allowed to freeze. If the ball is allowed to freeze too deeply, or to get too cold, root damage is possible. Root systems do not go dormant and may be subject to severe injury if exposed to extreme freezing temperatures in the root ball. Root-killing temperatures vary with species (see Chapter 8).

If the digging operation is interrupted, the pit should be mulched and covered to prevent further freezing. Trees should not be dug or transported when the daytime air temperature is below 20°F (-7°C). The root ball must be protected from thawing during the moving process or it could fall apart. Consequently, a frozen soil ball must be moved promptly to its new site and covered to prevent root injury and freeze drying of the outer surface.

The planting hole location should also be heavily mulched before the ground freezes or digging may be impossible. After the hole is dug, both the hole and the backfill soil should be mulched until the tree is planted.

Burlapping and lacing

Soil balls are wrapped with burlap and twine to support the root ball during transport. It is important that the burlap and twine are very tight and secure. Use only natural fiber materials. Synthetic materials have caused the death of plants in the landscape when not removed. Some natural fiber materials are chemically treated to render them resistant to decay, and even these may persist too long after planting under some circumstances (see Chapter 7).

Small soil balls are undercut easily with a spade and then lifted from the hole before wrapping with burlap. The ball is placed on the center of a piece of burlap so that the diagonal corners of the burlap can be pulled tightly across the top of the ball and tied securely. The loose folds can be tightened around the ball by pleating and pinning them tightly with nails (Figure 6-5). These small soil balls are usually wrapped with twine to strengthen and stabilize them.

Machine-dug trees are sometimes placed directly into wire baskets lined with burlap. The baskets can be ordered in many sizes, and final tightening around the root ball can be easily accomplished with the twist of a hook. The top of the soil ball is tied closed with twine (Figure 6-6). This system provides excellent support for the root ball, but the basket does not rust away for many years after planting and should be at least partially removed (see Chapter 7).

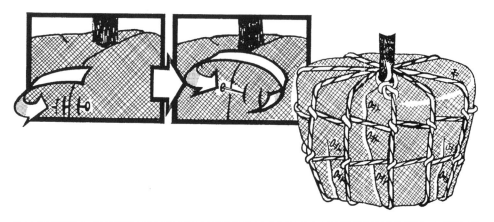

FIGURE 6-5.   Nails are inserted in one direction, then used as a lever and turned and pushed in the opposite direction, thus pulling the burlap tight and holding it in place. The root ball is wrapped with twine to strengthen and support it.

FIGURE 6-6.   Wire baskets are sometimes used to support the soil ball.

The sides and top of larger root balls are wrapped and laced while still in the hole before undercutting. Burlap pieces 1 ft (30 cm) wider than the depth of the ball should be laid around the ball, flush with the bottom and extending over the top at least 1 ft (30 cm). Overlapping strips and folds should be pinned in place. Drum lacing and top lacing provides the extra support needed by larger root balls (Figure 6-7). Cash (150) suggested a more extensive top-lacing. Smaller soil balls of sandy or loose soil may also require this technique.

Very large balls of sandy or loose soil may require double wrapping with burlap, and the bottom of the ball may need to be wrapped and bottom-laced after breaking the ball loose. If the tree is to be transported in a horizontal position, the top of the ball should be wrapped and top-laced. A layer of wire fencing or stiff wire cloth can be used to wrap the ball in addition to rope lacing to provide additional support (Figure 6-8).

Breaking ball free or undercutting

A sharp spade can be used to undercut root balls up to about 3 ft (1 m) diameter, but the ball may have to be tipped somewhat to reach the center with the spade. Root balls over 15 in (38 cm) cannot be undercut without some movement of the root ball and must be burlapped and laced first to prevent the root ball from breaking.

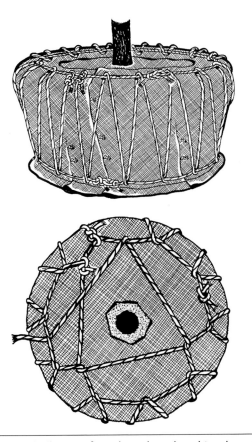

FIGURE 6-7. Large root balls are often drum laced and top laced for extra support.

FIGURE 6-8. Large soil balls are sometimes wrapped with wire cloth for extra support. The wire must be removed during the planting process.

Under most soil conditions, direct lifting of large soil balls will break the bottom of the soil ball free, even if all bottom roots have not been severed. If necessary, large soil balls may be undercut by running a small steel cable around the bottom of the ball below the burlap and securing both ends to a hook on the end of another cable running to a winch. When power is applied, the cable cuts underneath the ball, severing all small roots. A second procedure for undercutting the bottom of the ball is to anchor one end of a cable securely to a steel bar anchored at the bottom of the hole, looping the cable around the base of the ball and then through a slit trench to a power winch. When the power is applied to the cable, the loop applies even pressure as it cuts through the base of the ball. Care must be taken to keep the pulling end of the cable as low as possible in the hole in order to obtain a level cut across the bottom of the soil ball. Two heavy steel pry bars can be used to hold the cable down. When large roots are encountered, undercutting can be done by placing a choker cable at the base of the ball and working the cable through the soil with the aid of an articulated tractor.

Moving the soil ball

It may take more than one person to lift even a small ball. **A plant should never be lifted from the hole by the stem.** Heavier balls can be lifted from the standing position by using a sling or straps. Plants weighing up to 500 lb (225 kg) can be moved short distances on a hand pushcart (Figure 6-9). Moving larger balls, or small root balls longer distances, will require powered equipment. Fork lifts and bucket loaders are often used, but can cause damage to the soil ball and tree trunk. Several kinds of specialized equipment and accessories for conventional power equipment are available for lifting root balls (Figure 6-10).

FIGURE 6-9. Handcarts are useful for moving small plants. Many designs are available commercially.

FIGURE 6-10. Several kinds of specialized equipment and accessories for conventional equipment are available for lifting root balls.

In-ground fabric bags

Plants growing in fabric bags in the field may be dug with a hand spade. For greater efficiency, large numbers of plants can be pulled out of the ground with specialized tractor-mounted equipment (164). The root balls are transported in the bags, with no additional wrapping. The top of the bag is sometimes laced together with twine. The bags must be removed before planting. Growers may remove the bag and replace it with burlap or a container before shipping to make the plant more appealing to the buyer, especially for retail merchants.

Balled and potted (Containerized)

Another method of handing field-grown nursery stock is the balled and potted system. In this method, plants are dug with a ball of earth and then placed immediately into a container. Plants grown in in-ground fabric bags are sometimes potted before sale. In temperate climates the plants are usually dug in early spring or early fall, potted, and sold after the plant has had a chance to adjust to the stress of transplanting (4-6 weeks) (154). In warmer climates, plants are dug while dormant and sold after the roots have filled the media inside the container.

Field potting is also feasible during the hot summer months after plants have made their initial flush of growth. Ideally these plants should be dug early in the morning, potted, and moved immediately to a shady holding area with overhead sprinkler irrigation. The plants should be held in this area until sufficient root regeneration occurs and leaves remain turgid throughout the day.

Storage

If plants are not to be replanted immediately, special storage conditions are required, both at the nursery and the planting site. If cared for properly, plants with soil balls can be stored (heeled-in) for several months without damage (Figure 6-11). This allows nurseries to dig plants in the spring and have them available throughout the season. The plants are placed in an area with good surface drainage and covered with a loose, damp medium to help keep the root ball moist. Composted wood chips or sawdust are often used for this purpose. Because decomposition of fresh wood chips, and especially sawdust, can produce a large amount of heat, provision must be made for regular watering, if and when temperatures in the mulch approach 90°F (32°C).

For long-term storage, partial shade and an irrigation system are beneficial. A **dilute** solution of a soluble fertilizer should be applied to the soil balls two or three times during the growing season. A bed of wood chips and sawdust settles rapidly. Additional mulch may have to be added from time to time to keep the root balls covered. Evergreen plants in Florida are often dug in winter (late December though March). The root ball is watered several times during the day for several weeks (up to 2 months on larger plants), and then only once a day until the plants are sold throughout the year. Overhead irrigation may not be needed if this procedure is followed, especially for live oak (*Quercus virginiana*) and laurel oak (*Quercus laurifolia*).

If mulched-in for several months, roots may begin to grow 6-12 in (15-30 cm) or more out of the root ball and into the mulch. The natural tendency is to try to

FIGURE 6-11. Ball and burlap plants being stored until needed for planting. Closely spaced plants help to protect each other from sun and wind exposure. Trickle irrigation is being used to keep root balls moist.

preserve all new root growth when the plant is moved, but doing so may be problematic. When the plant is moved, the mulch will fall away and the roots will be exposed. To preserve the roots, they will have to be wrapped with another layer of burlap, bending them at a sharp angle and pressing them against the surface of the root ball. The roots should not be left in this position. It will be difficult to position them back in their original orientation and fill around them with soil at the planting site, resulting in kinked or circling roots. It may be best to prune off the new roots before planting.

Hardening-off is a more intensive, but shorter-term procedure than heeling-in. It is used to acclimate plants to root loss and to minimize transpiration and water stress when they are dug with foliage in summer. Plants dug from the field in-leaf continue to transpire at a high rate for at least a few days before adjusting (165). In addition to heeling-in the root ball with wood chips and irrigating to keep it moist, ideally the foliage should be shaded, shielded from wind, and sprinkled frequently with water during daylight hours. It may be necessary to harden-off plants for up to 2 weeks to be sure plants will survive summer digging.

Shipping

Trees are often too tall to be transported in the upright position and must be tipped to a horizontal position. When trees are being loaded on a truck or trailer bed for shipping, they have to be secured, but care must be taken to avoid injuring the tree or breaking the soil ball. The trunk and branches should be padded with several thickness' of burlap to prevent bruising wherever contact is made.

Plants should be covered when transported on an open bed (Figure 6-12). Even dormant plants and their root balls can be desiccated when transported uncovered at highway speeds. Covering is absolutely imperative when plants are transported with leaves. A saran cloth tarp will protect foliage from wind while driving. Be careful to avoid heat build-up under the tarp while parked in the sun. In warm weather, plants in leaf should be covered immediately before being transported, and the cover should be removed immediately after arriving at the destination.

Wrapping the root balls in plastic "shrink wrap" keeps the root ball soil from drying out during shipping (Edward Gilman, personal communication). The importance of keeping the soil ball moist during and after shipping cannot be stressed too strongly. It is easy to forget that soil balls may arrive at the planting site dry if it has been a few days since they were dug at the nursery. Inspect plants thoroughly when received.

MECHANICAL TREE SPADES

There are many models of tree spades designed for moving trees with trunks 4-9 in (10-22 cm) in diameter. These machines are similar to the mechanical diggers used in the nursery, but these truck-mounted tree spades are designed to dig, transport, and replant the tree directly into the landscape (Figure 6-13). Tree spades are expensive, specialized pieces of equipment that require training and experience to operate. Usually a firm owning the equipment will be contracted to move the trees.

FIGURE 6-12. Cover plants when transporting them on an open bed, even when they are dormant.

FIGURE 6-13. Tree spades are available in many sizes. This large tree spade, which digs a root ball 90 inches in diameter, is the largest manufactured tree spade.

If the job calls for only a few trees and the distance between the nursery and planting site is short, it is often economical to use a tree spade. Tree spades are often used to remove plants that have outgrown their space in the landscape because it is quick and leaves minimal disturbance. The size and weight of the truck and soil ball may limit access to some areas. Tree spades cannot usually be used on hillsides. Low, spreading branches can also prevent the use of a tree spade.

The same ratio of tree caliper to ball size should be followed as for other methods of digging soil balls. As with other transplanting methods, the tree should be covered while in transit. Since the trees are usually only transported a short distance, and the root ball is constantly supported by the spades throughout the process, success rates for trees moved with a tree spade in-leaf are usually very good. Trees dug in-leaf cannot be hardened-off before planting in the landscape using this method, so special care may be needed after planting.

PALMS

Palm trees are not woody plants. They do not have a cambium and are not capable of generating new tissue to cover injured areas. Avoid any mechanical damage to the trunks of palms. Terminal buds of palms must be carefully protected from damage, since it is only from this structure that new growth develops.

Digging

Palms are often moved with very small soil balls (Figure 6-14). When the sandy soils are allowed to fall off the roots that do remain, the method might be better

FIGURE 6-14. Palms are often moved with very small root balls. (photo credit - E. Gilman)

described as bare root. For cabbage palms *(Sabal palmetto)* and other species that regenerate all of their new roots from the base of the trunk instead of the severed root ends, this may be acceptable. Other palms would benefit from more typical root ball procedures. See Chapter 8 for more detail on palm root regeneration. Large multi-stemmed palms may require a ball of 10 to 12 ft diameter.

Storage

Palms not immediately replanted should be heeled-in like any other plant. Transferring palms to containers is another good way to hold plants. Irrigation and protection from excess sun are important.

Transporting

Some or all of the palm leaves are often removed prior to transport, rather than waiting to prune them at the planting site. The proper method varies with species and circumstances (see Chapter 7).

Palms are lifted in most instances by means of a strap or sling placed just above the estimated balance point on the trunk. The small size and weight of the root ball offers no logical means of lifting by the ball. Nylon slings should be used because they offer a high degree of protection for the palm trunk. When a sling is being attached to the trunk, the surface must be protected from burn or compression marks that will form permanent scars.

When many single-stemmed palms are to be transported, they can be literally laid flat or shingled on a flat-bed trailer. The tops should always be tied securely.

Transplanted palms with long slender trunks should have a supporting timber attached to its trunk during transport. This important protective support is justified because the alternative is the possible loss of the essential terminal bud and the ultimate death of the palm.

LARGE TREES

Before modern heavy equipment was available to handle the weight of large root balls, trees 15 in (38 cm) and greater were moved bare root (157). Today, large trees are moved with a soil ball that requires extensive knowledge of both horticulture and heavy equipment. Several accounts of moving large trees have been published (153,158,161,162,163,166,168). Mature size trees have been moved successfully, but the cost is very high, and it may take decades for them to fully establish on the new site (see Chapter 9).

Special procedures are often used to minimize water stress of large transplanted trees. Proper root pruning prior to transplanting can help to minimize water stress (see Chapter 5). Thinning the crown to reduce transpirational water loss is also sometimes practiced. Some contractors install sprinkler heads throughout the crown after planting to cool the foliage and reduce transpiration. Research on small trees suggests this practice may be necessary for only a few weeks (147,149).

Trees small enough to use standard B&B root ball procedures (12 in (30 cm) dbh) are moved with commonly available equipment such as winch trucks and cranes. Special chain harnesses are usually needed to support and lift larger root balls. Experienced contractors who do a lot of this work (Figure 4-1) own winch trucks specially designed for tree moving. Cranes can be easily rented but may be expensive and require a skilled operator (Figure 6-15). For trees of this size, neither the weight of the root ball nor the size of the crown after tying should exceed road limits and prohibit transport from site to site.

In special situations, trees have been moved by direct lift from the trunk. The method is sometimes preferred in sandy soils where root balls may break if the tree is lifted by the root ball alone. In this method, one or two heavy steel pins are inserted in holes drilled through the trunk. These pins are used to lift the tree in the upright position using a crane (Figure 6-16). It is best to lift the tree by both the pins in the trunk and by the root ball. The drawback of this method is the injury to the trunk, especially the introduction of decay through the wounds.

The largest existing tree spade digs a 14 ft (4.25 m) diameter root ball. It is one-of-a-kind and has been used in locations around the United States (Figure 6-17). Because of the difficulty and cost of transporting this machine, it is probably only realistic to use this machine on large jobs with many trees to move.

FIGURE 6-15. Cranes are often used to lift large trees. (photo credit - T. Thornhill)

FIGURE 6-16. Special devices are sometimes used to hold the root balls of large trees. Pins inserted in holes drilled through the trunk are also sometimes used to lift trees in the upright position using a crane. Potential injury to the tree limits the use of these pins to only those situations where no other method will work. (photo credit - Civic Trees)

FIGURE 6-17. This largest tree spade ever built digs a root ball 14 ft (4.25 m) in diameter. This is a one-of-a-kind custom machine. (photo credit - T. Thornhill)

Trees too large to move with conventional root balls are often moved in boxes constructed around a square root ball. The boxing method requires much specialized knowledge and equipment and is presently done by only a small number of contractors. First an oversized square root ball is dug with a trencher or backhoe. After final shaping and root pruning with hand tools, the sides of the box are constructed with hardwood planks. The second phase is to dig underneath the root ball and install planks for the bottom of the box. This can be very dangerous and should only be done by qualified contractors. The top of the root ball is sometimes also covered with planks. The box lifts the tree.

Large boxed trees are usually transported in the upright position because of their great size and weight. Height and width of the crown, as well as weight of root ball, may require special permits restricting where they can be moved. Utility wires and light poles may have to be moved. This is a job for an experienced contractor. When the tree is planted, the sides of the box will be removed, but the bottom will remain in place.

Moving mature trees

Though not commonplace, very large mature trees have been transplanted. Root balls can weigh from 100 to 500 tons, and crowns can be up to 80 ft (53 m) tall and just as wide. There are very few contractors that are capable of moving trees of this size. Trees must be root pruned in advance, preferably in stages starting 2-3 years before the tree is boxed and moved. Lifting a very large tree and its root ball requires very specialized equipment and techniques. Sometimes cranes lift them by both root ball and the branches. Tensions must be even on all cables to avoid damaging branches. Using the sound made by the cable when struck with a hammer to judge cable tension (like tuning a piano string) is an example of the very specialized methods used by experienced contractors. The heaviest trees may have to be lifted with gantries (Figure 6-18). Special trailers with over 100 wheels are used to distribute the load (Figure 6-19). Each wheel has a separate hydraulic leveler to keep the tree perfectly vertical at all times and independent steering to maneuver in difficult places. These large trees may be too wide for roadways or too heavy for bridges, and are usually not moved very far. Extremely large trees (up to 500 tons) can be moved with a crawler-transporter (Figure 6-20). The weight and size of the plant as well as the requirement for relatively level terrain limits where this equipment can be used.

FIGURE 6-18. Gantries being used to lift a very large tree with the root ball supported by a wooden box. (photo credit - T. Thornhill)

FIGURE 6-19. A very large boxed tree on a special trailer with over 100 wheels and special leveling and steering systems. (photo credit - T. Thornhill)

FIGURE 6-20. A huge tree on crawler-transporter (note man standing by treads). (photo credit - T. Thornhill)

Once at the new location, it is likely that the entire site will have to be constructed around the new tree. The tree will usually be set at a predetermined elevation, with soil filled around and under the "root ball" to bring it to final grade (Figure 6-21).

Because of the size and weight, very large trees are often moved in summer or winter when the ground is dry or frozen. The trees have already been root pruned up to several years in advance to help minimize stress. The trees will essentially be deriving moisture from the root ball whether at the new site or old. The rigid boxes and sophisticated lifting systems probably result in less root ball shifting (fine root loss) than B&B trees. Excellent post-planting care is always part of such a major project. Considering these factors, moving trees in summer is not a major concern.

Guarantee

A guarantee may not be offered on large trees, but individual contractors may have different policies. A one-year guarantee may have some value in case of a complete failure, but the first year is not usually the problem. Since it takes many years, or even decades for the largest trees to establish, the majority of transplant

FIGURE 6-21. A large tree at its new site before soil is filled in around it. (photo credit - T. Thornhill)

failures may occur several years after transplanting when diligent maintenance seems less important and watering is reduced for the tree that is only partially established. The tree may then decline slowly over many years without an obvious reason. Do not move trees larger than 12 in (30 cm.) in diameter if you are not prepared to provide regular irrigation for **many** years.

CONTAINER PLANTS

Hardening-off, heeling-in, and other long-term storage concerns are not an issue with container-grown plants, since they are not usually moved from the nursery growing area until they are shipped. However, shipping and storage conditions at the receiving end are of concern. When plants arrive at the planting site, they require irrigation once or twice daily. Since soil-less container media is well drained and frequently irrigated in the nursery, the container plants will also have to be watered frequently after leaving the nursery to avoid drought stress.

Trees and shrubs must arrive at the planting site in excellent condition. Reject plants with broken or undersized root balls, container plants with circling roots, plants with injury from rough treatment and plants that have been drought stressed. Plant only the highest quality material for the best chance of success.

LITERATURE CITED

145. Anonymous. 1989. British Standard Recommendations for Transplanting Root-balled Trees. British Standards Institution. 11 pp.
146. Anonymous. 1996. American Standard for Nursery Stock. American Association of Nurserymen. Washington, D.C., 57 pp.
147. Bates, R.M. and A.X. Niemiera. 1994. *Mist irrigation reduces post-transplant desiccation of bare-root trees.* J. Environ. Hort. 12:1-3.
148. Bates, R.M. and A.X. Niemiera. 1996. *Effect of transplanting on shoot water potential of bare-root Washington hawthorn and Norway maple.* J. Environ. Hort. 14:1-4.
149. Beeson R.C. and E.F. Gilman. 1992. *Water stress and osmotic adjustment during post-digging acclimation of* Quercus virginiana *produced in fabric containers.* J. Environ. Hort. 10:208-214.
150. Cash, R.C. 1990. *Ball lacing: an examination of the methods.* J. Arboric. 16:66-68.
151. Chen, T.H.H., P. Murakami, P. Lombard, and L.H. Fuchigami. 1991. *Desiccation tolerance in bare-rooted apple trees prior to transplanting.* J. Environ. Hort. 9:13-17.
152. Cleary, B. and R. Tinus. 1980. *Preservation of nursery stock quality through packaging storage, transport and planting.* N.Z. J. For. Sci. 10:295-296.
153. Cohen, L. 1987. *How do you move a large tree?* Landscape Contractor (September): 8-9.
154. Davidson, H., R. Mecklenburg, and C. Peterson. 1988. Nursery management. Prentice Hall, Englewood Cliffs, NJ. 413 pp.
155. Englert, J.M., L.H. Fuchigami, and T.H.H. Chen. 1993. *Effects of storage temperatures and duration on the performances of bare-root deciduous hardwood trees.* J. Arboric. 19:106-112.
156. Englert, J.M., K. Warren, L. Fuchigami, and T.H.H. Chen. 1993 *Antidesiccant compounds improve the survival of bare-root deciduous nursery trees.* Am. Soc. Hort. Sci. 118:228-235.
157. Flemer, W. III. 1967. *Is bare-root transplanting a dying art?* Am. Nurseryman 126(1): 24-25, 185-193.
158. Irish, E.E. 1976. *Transplanting large trees.* J. Arboric. 2:173-175.
159. McCracken, I.J. 1978. *Carbon dioxide uptake of pine seedlings after cold storage.* For. Sci. 24:17-25.
160. Murakami, P., T.H.H. Chen, and L.H. Fuchigami. 1990. *Desiccation tolerance of deciduous plants during postharvest handling.* J. Environ. Hort. 8:22-25.
161. Newman, C.J. 1982. *English techniques in large tree transplanting.* J. Arboric. 8:90-93.
162. O'Callaghan, D.P.O. 1989. *Transplanting a mature cutleaf basswood in Preston, England.* J. Arboric. 15(3): 5.
163. Rae, W.A. 1976. *Tree transplanting.* J. Arboric. 2:133-135.

164. Reiger, R. and C. Whitcomb. 1984. *A root control system for growing and transplanting trees.* J. Arboric. 9:33-38.

165. Rook, D.A. 1973. *Conditioning* radiata *pine seedlings to transplanting by restricted watering.* N. Z. J. For. Sci. 3:54-69.

166. Shaw, D.C. 1980. *Moving large trees.* J. Arboric. 6:51-52.

167. Webb, D.P. 1977. *Root regeneration and bud dormancy of sugar maple, silver maple and white ash seedlings: effects of chilling.* For. Sci. 23:474-483.

168. Webb, R. 1995. *Moving mature banyan trees in Hong Kong.* J. Arboric. 19:339-347.

chapter

7

Planting

Planting is much more than putting the plant in the hole and surrounding the roots with soil. First, you must evaluate and prepare the site correctly, decide when to plant, choose the proper plant, and make sure it arrives at the planting site in good condition. Only then is it time to plant.

PREPARING TO PLANT

Proper planting depth

Planting too deeply is the most common mistake made during planting, and it is nearly impossible to correct when discovered several months, or years, later. Symptoms of poor vigor and slow growth often result from planting too deep. Collar rot and basal canker diseases have been reported on sugar maple (*Acer saccharum*) many years after planting too deep (187). Root depth should be checked, and rechecked, starting when selecting the plants from the nursery and one final time just before backfilling the planting hole. The original depth of the plant in the nursery can often be determined by observing a color difference on the trunk, but this may not be the best depth to replant it if it was already too deep in the nursery.

Bare root plants should be placed in a hole that is both wide enough and deep enough to accommodate the entire root system. Unusually long roots may be pruned back to the standard minimum spread in order to fit into the hole without bending (minimum root spread standards are listed in Table 5-1). The roots should be straightened to prevent kinking, crowding, and crossing of main roots. Lateral roots that could later girdle the main roots or trunk should be cut off with sharp pruning shears. Any damaged or diseased roots should be removed.

Select ball and burlap plants with the root flare at, or just below, the soil surface and dig the planting hole to the proper depth. If trees were not checked in the nursery for the presence of a root flare, do it before planting. It is not uncommon for the root flare to be too deep in the root ball (Figure 7-1). Serious errors in planting depth can result in failure. If the holes were pre-dug, check to be sure

FIGURE 7-1. It is not unusual for the roots to be confined to the bottom of the root ball when a tree is planted too deep in the nursery. Sometimes a few adventitious roots will form on the buried stem, but these are usually not enough to support the plant if the main roots die. Note the different color of the stem where it was buried.

that the depth of each hole and each root ball are the same before placing the heavy root ball in the hole. It is easy for both the hole and the soil ball depth to vary a couple of inches. Make final adjustments as necessary. After the plant is in the hole, make a final confirmation of the root flare location. This will require removing the twine and burlap from around the trunk. It may be necessary to make final adjustments before backfilling with soil. The plant may have to be rejected if a major problem is discovered, even at this late stage in the planting process.

Container plants should also be planted so that the top of the root ball is at grade. Always check to see that the first roots emerge from the stem near the soil surface. This is especially important for containerized plants that have been dug from the field and grown in containers for a few months, since they may not have been planted correctly or may have settled after planting.

Palm root balls are sometimes planted deeper to make heights more even, but it is recommended that for most palm species 2 in (5 cm) of root initiation zone (often visible as a portion of the trunk where roots form aboveground) remain above the soil line (199). Pygmy palms (*Phoenix roebelenii*) planted with the visible portion of the root initiation zone buried can grow as well as trees planted at original depth. When planted deeper, new roots may form up to 6 in (15 cm) above the root initiation zone, but tree survival is decreased (178).

Directional orientation

Root systems and crowns may develop asymmetrically in response to sun (237,241) and prevailing wind exposure. A tree should be oriented in the hole so that it faces the same compass direction as it did when it was growing in the nursery. Turning the tree may expose less-acclimatized bark from the shaded north side to direct sun. This is suspected of increasing the chances of sunscald, especially on thin, smooth-barked species. If the tree cannot be oriented as before, perhaps because of crown form, it is even more important to protect the trunk on thin barked trees from sunscald, as discussed later in this chapter.

Glazing and drying

Clay soils will glaze much more readily than loamy and sandy soils. Glazing can cause difficulties in some situations, but roots will usually grow easily through small unglazed areas, and cracks in the glaze. The glazing would have to be almost completely continuous to pose a serious barrier to root growth. Though partial glazing may not be a serious problem, it is best to eliminate the potential for trouble by using a hand tool to break up the glazed surface before planting. If holes are dug in advance, the soil surface may become dry and very hard on the surface. It is best to break up the dry surface to expose some moist soil before planting.

Root dips

Several types of synthetic gel or cornstarch based root dips designed to prevent desiccation of bare root stock are available. These root dips do not aid in establishment of some species when adequate soil moisture is available (173). Benefits are most likely to be derived from these compounds in drought or in low-maintenance situations (204).

Root ball wrappings

Materials used to cover and support the root ball serve a very useful purpose during transport of the plant material but serve no purpose once the root ball is in its final place in the planting hole. The reasons given by contractors for not removing the wrappings (or the critical portions of them) are not usually horticultural. The extra time it takes to remove them may increase the cost of planting, and it may be more difficult to straighten the tree without breaking the root ball if it begins to lean after planting. Thoroughly stabilizing the lower part of the root ball at planting will keep firm root balls from shifting, and they will usually not have to be straightened later.

It is often assumed that natural **burlap and twine** will decompose rapidly after planting. When left in place, they sometimes remain strong for several years — long enough to cause serious constriction of the basal trunk area. Burlap over the root ball can repel water and cause the root ball to dry out. Burlap and twine may decompose very slowly when exposed (Figure 7-2). Natural burlap is often treated with preservatives to prevent rapid decomposition. In one study, treated burlap showed little sign of decomposition in 2-3 years (216) and was also observed to persist up to 14 years. In the warm and moist soils of Florida it may take only a few months to decompose. As roots grow through the burlap and increase in diameter, they can be girdled by the burlap fibers (Figure 7-3). The plant cannot become established as long as the burlap is present to girdle the

FIGURE 7-2. When the root ball is planted correctly, the burlap and twine will be exposed if they are not removed. Exposed, burlap and twine decompose very slowly and could cause girdling at the base of the trunk. Remove them before back filling the hole.

FIGURE 7-3. The treated burlap on this root ball had not decomposed in two years (upper left) and it girdled the new roots growing through it (lower right).

new roots growing out of the root ball. Synthetic burlap does not decompose and roots will **never** develop normally when this material is left around the root ball. Synthetic twine that is not removed from the base of the tree will girdle the trunk (Figure 7-4) and cause death of the tree in a few years. Sometimes the trunk will break at the point of constriction. After the soil ball has been placed in the hole and stabilized by tamping soil firmly around the lower quarter of the root ball, cut off and remove the burlap and twine from the top and sides of the root ball, but not from beneath the ball (Figure 7-5).

When **wire baskets** were first introduced for supporting the root ball, it was assumed that they would rust away in a few years. **Wire baskets can last up to 30 years** (Watson, unpublished data). Usually, the top of the root flare roots grows into one of the upper horizontal wires (Figure 7-6, left). As the roots grow against these wires, the roots become partially girdled. Transport of water and nutrients to the trunk and carbohydrates to the rest of the root system are restricted (191). The root tissue may eventually grow around the wires and graft together on the other side (196,209,218,219), but it may take several years to reestablish unrestricted vascular transport (Figure 7-6, right). Flow of water and nutrients can be constricted in one or more of the major flare roots for many years, and the resulting chronic stress could lead to other problems. All potentially damaging portions of the wire basket should be removed at planting time. It is usually just the upper horizontal wires that interfere with root growth. Parts of the basket left protruding above ground could be a hazard. To prevent future problems, cut off the top half of the basket before backfilling (Figure 7-7).

In some parts of Europe, plastic baskets are used rather than wire baskets (193). They are very lightweight and are intended to break as the roots grow

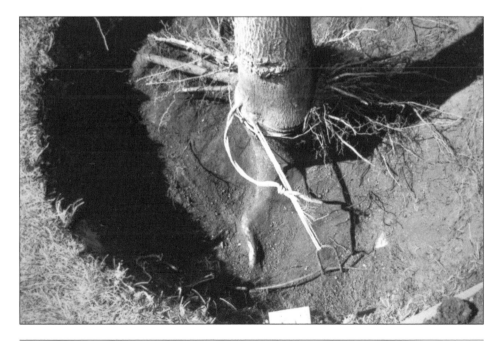

FIGURE 7-4. Nylon twine does not decompose and will girdle the base of the trunk if not removed.

FIGURE 7-5. Burlap and twine should be removed after the root ball has been placed in the hole. It no longer serves any useful purpose and can constrict the trunk and roots.

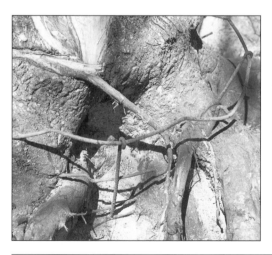

FIGURE 7-6. This wire basket did not rust in 30 years. Roots may eventually grow over the wires of baskets used to support root balls (left), but vascular flow can be interrupted for several years (right), leading to stress.

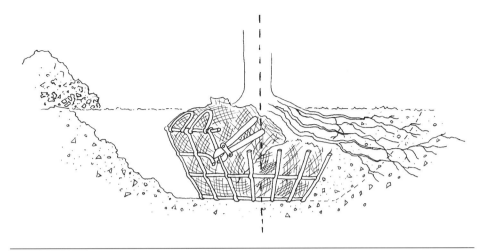

FIGURE 7-7. If the upper half of the basket is removed before backfilling, most future root problems will be prevented.

against them. There are no published reports of what effects plastic baskets may have on future root development.

Disrupting circling roots

Though many techniques have been developed to prevent roots from circling around the inside of containers, the problem is still frequently encountered in the landscape. It is common practice to cut these circling roots on the surface of the root ball by making several vertical cuts, or "slashes", on the outside of the root ball before planting. Another technique that is useful on small plants, called "butterflying", involves a single deep cut through the bottom of the root ball. The two halves are then spread open and placed against the bottom of the planting hole (Figure 7-8). Both of these techniques cause root injury and could lead to increased stress after planting, but reports are conflicting (172,174,188,195,220). Moderate stress from disrupting the circling roots is preferable to allowing circling roots to persist.

Though superficial circling roots on the surface of a container root ball can be corrected by slashing or butterflying, additional circling roots may also be present deep within the root ball if the plant was grown in smaller pots during earlier stages of production (Figure 5-13). Butterflying the root ball may also disrupt interior circling roots if they are not too high in the root ball.

BACKFILLING

On sites with soil of high quality, it is doubtful that the backfill will require amending. Amendments may have to be considered on some sites to improve soil structure, water-holding capacity, or drainage (see Chapter 3).

When refilling the planting hole, the backfill soil should be free of clumps. The first lateral roots of bare root stock should be planted within approximately 1 in

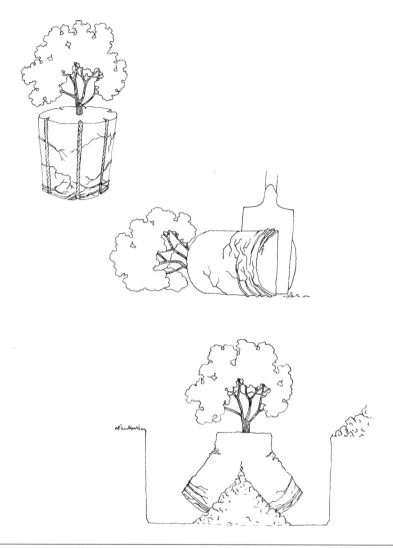

FIGURE 7-8. Slashing (left) and butterflying (right) a container root ball to disrupt circling roots.

(2.5 cm) of the soil surface. While holding the plant in the correct position, add loose soil around the roots and tamp it lightly until no air pockets remain, without causing the plant to settle deeper in the hole. Add water to settle the soil around the roots, and then add more soil if necessary. Check again to be sure that the first lateral roots are just below the soil surface.

The backfill soil can be tamped firmly around the base of the root ball to stabilize it, but the rest of the soil should be tamped only lightly, or left to settle on its own. Soaking will assist in settling the soil naturally. **Excessive tamping can compact soil and slow water penetration and root growth.** The soil can be mounded slightly between the root ball and the edge of the planting hole to allow for settling, but do not cover the root ball with soil. The root ball surface was the soil surface in the nursery and should not be buried. If water is expected to percolate slowly in the soil, or if the planting site is not level, a raised ring of soil can be formed around the edge of the root ball to create a basin that can be filled with water (Figure 7-9).

Trees transplanted with tree spades require special procedures. The fit between the root ball and the sides of the hole is never perfect. Wide spaces and air pockets often occur, especially if the hole is slightly shallower than the root ball or the root ball was rotated slightly. The root ball will eventually settle and close the open space around the root ball, but this could take time. While the spaces are open, roots will not be able to regenerate, and the soil ball will dry out. Use a hand spade or shovel to loosen the soil around the edge of the root ball, and fill the spaces with loose, friable soil. A better procedure would be to cultivate the soil 12 in (30 cm) deep for several feet around the root ball. This will also encourage rapid growth of new roots (171,175). You may still have to use a spade, fork, or a stream of water to work the loose soil into the gap around the root ball.

PRUNING AT PLANTING

There is no single correct way to prune trees and shrubs at planting time. If pruning was done correctly during production in the nursery, the plant may require very little pruning at planting except for removing small broken twigs or branches. Other plants may need considerable pruning. Properly trained young trees should require minimal corrective pruning as they mature.

Pruning to totally compensate for root loss is not possible. Recommendations sometimes call for removing 20 to 30 percent of the branches and leaves, but a tree can loose as much as 95 percent of its root system during transplanting. Most studies indicate that moderate crown pruning at planting has little or no effect on the growth of roots or shoots (189,190,198,211,230,231,234). When a tree is

FIGURE 7-9.   A raised ring of soil formed around the edge of the root ball to create a basin that can be filled with water.

planted during the dormant season, the new leaves that later develop will usually expand less because of the reduced water supply from the roots (214). A plant dug in summer will have a crown of full-sized leaves when root loss occurs, and will be less able to adjust to the sudden stress. More severe pruning may be appropriate to reduce transpiration. It is possible to prune too much and either destroy the natural shape of the plant, or reduce photosynthesis to such an extent that growth is greatly reduced.

Making proper pruning cuts

When removing a live branch, pruning cuts should be made just outside the branch collar (Figure 7-10). If no collar is visible, the angle of the cut should approximate the angle formed by the branch bark ridge and the trunk. Flush cuts make larger wounds, increase decay, and should be avoided.

Stubs and rough wood callus over slowly and are more susceptible to fungal and bacterial infections. Tearing the bark on large limbs can be avoided by using a standard three-cut procedure (169).

Wound dressings

Wound dressings and tree paints have not been shown to be effective in preventing or reducing decay. They are not usually recommended for routine use on pruning cuts unless specified for control of disease, borers, mistletoe, or sprouts. In some areas of the United States and during certain seasons, wound dressings are beneficial in preventing invasion of certain vascular fungi, such as *Verticillium* and *Ceratocystis*, as well as weakly pathogenic canker fungi. Wound dressings are sometimes used to reduce drying back of the inner bark and cambium, and to prevent deep weather checking due to drying of the inner wood. Recent research indicates that certain wound dressings (212) and wrapping wounds with polyethylene plastic wrap (221) may reduce dieback of uninjured cambium and promote wound closure.

FIGURE 7-10.   Pruning cuts should be made just outside the branch bark ridge (top of cut) and the collar (bottom of cut)

Pruning multi-stem shrubs

All injured, weak, interfering, and poorly placed branches should be removed at the time of planting. Pruning may require the complete removal of older stems and the shortening of newer ones. New shoots from the base of the plant should be encouraged to replace older stems that are removed. Shearing is appropriate only where a hedge or other extremely formal appearance is required.

Though not often practiced, rejuvenation pruning can be used on transplanted shrubs. When all the stems are cut to 4-6 in (10-15 cm) above the ground at the same time, a new top will reestablish quickly. This procedure may increase survival if maintenance after planting will be minimal. Not all species tolerate this type of pruning. Single stem shrubs should be pruned similarly to small trees.

Pruning evergreens

Most narrow- and broad-leaved evergreens require little pruning at planting time if they were properly pruned in the nursery. If possible, pruning should be restricted to 1-year-old wood. The growth habits of evergreens influence pruning practices. Fir (*Abies* sp.), pine (*Pinus* sp.), and spruce (*Picea* sp.) develop characteristic whorls of branches. Most of the growth occurs from closely placed buds near the end of the previous year's growth. Pruning can eliminate these buds, and they may have few or no latent buds, resulting in permanent disfiguration of the plant.

Arborvitae, false cypress, hemlock, juniper, and yew readily break lateral buds and, if necessary, can be moderately pruned before new growth appears. The terminals should be pruned back to a lateral branch, but the natural form of the plant should be maintained. Corrective pruning should be completed early in the spring before new growth develops because the new growth will help to cover the exposed inner branches.

Broadleaf evergreens should be pruned only to remove injured branches or to develop good branch structure. Heavy pruning is not recommended until after the first growing season, or later if the plants have not recovered well.

Pruning deciduous trees

Broken, weak, or interfering branches should be removed, as well as branches with included bark. Typical form for the species should be maintained (Figure 7-11). Trees of excurrent (strong central leader) growth habit usually need little or no training. The terminal leader should never be pruned from these trees. If the terminal has been accidentally broken, it should be pruned only as far as the next strong lateral twig or bud that can form the new terminal leader. Some **temporary** support may be required to train a new central leader.

Branch structure of large-growing decurrent (round-headed) trees can be improved by pruning when they are young. If possible, branches below the first permanent branch should be removed before they are 1/2 in (13 mm) in diameter to avoid large scars. The permanent branches should be evenly distributed around the trunk and spaced 12-18 in (45 cm) apart, though to reach this separation, the thinning process may be ongoing for 5 years or more after planting.

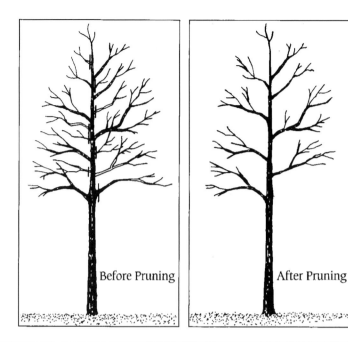

FIGURE 7-11. Broken, weak, and interfering branches should be removed at the time of planting. Maintain the typical form of the species.

Branches growing directly above one another should be no closer than 40-60 in (100-150 cm) on medium- to large-sized trees.

For strong attachment to the trunk, branches should be no more than one-half of the diameter of the trunk measured immediately above the branch attachment, with no included bark. If a branch is too large in relation to the trunk, selectively thin the branch, particularly near its terminal. This will reduce the weight of the branch, slow its growth, and develop a stronger branch attachment (169,194).

Pruning palms

In the past, it has been common practice to remove two-thirds or more of the leaves of palms before or just after transplanting (Figure 7-12). Removing all of the leaves of unirrigated sabal palm (*Sabal palmetto*) resulted in 95 percent survival after 8 months, compared to 64 percent survival when one-third of the leaves were left on the plant. All of the leaves left on the palms died within one to two months (176). Later work with pygmy date palms (*Phoenix roebelenii*) revealed a direct relationship to water stress. With regular irrigation, palm quality and root growth was increased as the number of leaves retained was increased. Under water stress conditions, the reverse was true. Tying the remaining leaves into a bundle to protect the bud from drying had no positive effect, and could lead to fungal infection in the bud if irrigation or rainfall were frequent (177).

A current recommendation for species where no specific research data is available is to remove no more than one-third of the leaves if the plant is moved with a small root ball. It is not necessary to remove any leaves of palms grown

FIGURE 7-12.   Two-thirds of the leaves are typically removed from palms at transplanting, and the remaining leaves are often tied over the terminal bud. Recent research shows that this may not be necessary.

in containers or moved with a tree spade. **If generous irrigation is provided, leaves do not need to be removed on any palm, regardless of transplant method.** If palm leaves are pruned off before moving the plant, additional leaf removal may not be necessary at the planting site.

SUPPORT SYSTEMS

Staking, guying, or bracing refers to the method of mechanically supporting the trunk of a planted tree to keep it in an upright position (201). Staking is both expensive and time consuming and may present a hazard for people who may trip or fall over the supports. Staking too rigidly can reduce trunk taper on small trees. Small trees may be too weak to stay upright on their own when the stake is removed (199). If the wires are left in place too long, the trunk can be girdled. Do not use a support system unless it is necessary, and then all supports should be removed after a reasonable period and before any trunk girdling can occur.

Bare root trees, fabric bag, and container-grown trees with small, lightweight root balls may require support until lateral or anchor roots develop, but seldom more than one year. Large evergreens may need to be guyed for up to two years because of the high wind resistance of the foliage and extra weight of snow and ice accumulation during the winter when the soil is wet. Extremely windy climates, or other unusual circumstances, may also call for extensive use of stakes.

When staking is needed to keep a tree with a strong, straight trunk in the upright position until the roots can grow to anchor the tree, low staking can keep the tree in place while permitting the top to move freely. If the trunk is weak, support the tree with a stake about 6 in (15 cm) above the lowest level at which the trunk can be held upright (199).

A single stake is often used on small trees. A single stake should be placed on the side of the tree toward the prevailing winds so the tree is blown away from the stake. Two stakes, with separate flexible ties is usually recommended (199). It is often easier to install stakes before the hole is backfilled. Guy wires are used on larger trees. The guys are best secured by specially designed land anchors or deadmen buried in the soil, and they should be at a 45-degree angle with the trunk (Figure 7-13). Galvanized steel cable is best. Turnbuckles can be installed to adjust the length. Compression springs can provide flexibility for trunk movement.

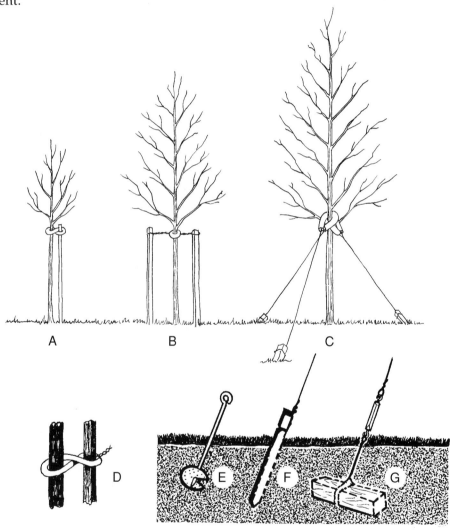

FIGURE 7-13.   Three methods of staking and guying trees. A. Single stake used for trees up to 2 in (5 cm) in diameter. The tree is attached to the stake by means of a wire run through a piece of hose (D). B. Trees 2 to 4 in (5 to 10 cm) in diameter are supported by two or three stakes. Attachment is the same as in A, and the stakes should be placed so the branches do not rub against them. C. Trees over 4 in (10 cm) in diameter should be guyed with at least three guys. Cable or wire is attached to the tree by running wires through a piece of hose or by using lag hooks on large trees. The guys should be secured to arrowhead-shaped land anchors (E), wooden stakes (F), or deadmen buried in the soil (G).

Many types of materials can be used to stake trees. Wooden stakes may still be the most popular, but metal pipes and fence stakes or poles are also used. The traditional material for tying the trees to the stakes is a wire slipped through a piece of garden hose, but this may sometimes cause damage. Many ties and support systems can be purchased specially for this purpose. It is important that the tying device be able to resist breaking and unfastening while allowing the tree trunk to flex. To prevent injury to the bark, the ties should be examined at least once during the growing season and adjusted if necessary.

Large palms are commonly supported after planting. Palms should be propped or guyed. However, nails, screws, and other mechanical devices must not be placed into the trunk. A common method of bracing or guying is to strap short, vertical pieces of 2 in x 4 in (5 cm x 10 cm) boards around the trunk with steel bands. The boards serve as supports in which to anchor screw eyes for guy wires, or to attach angled support braces (Figure 7-14).

Underground guying is sometimes necessary. A wooden frame is placed over the top of the root ball and held in place by cables anchored at the bottom of the planting hole by deadmen or specially designed land anchors. Once the cables are tightened and the hole is filled with soil the tree will be stabilized (Figure 7-15).

Stakes sometimes double as guards. Presumably, this is why some are so oversized (Figure 7-16). Specially designed trunk guards and grates are often installed to prevent vandalism and to cover planting pits. Both can eventually interfere with the growth of the tree (Figure 7-17). While they might be necessary in high traffic areas, they may need to be enlarged or removed as the tree grows in size.

FIGURE 7-14. Palms are often braced by strapping small boards to the trunk that serve as a place to anchor the angled wooden braces. Nails and screws must never be driven into the trunk of palms.

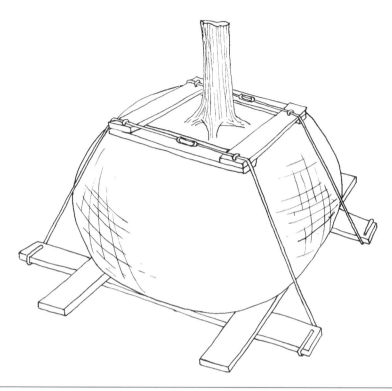

FIGURE 7-15. Underground guying can provide support for the tree without interfering with traffic or appearance above ground.

FIGURE 7-16. Tree stakes can also serve as guards to protect the tree from vandalism and accidents.

FIGURE 7-17. Planting pit grates often cause injury to the tree as it grows. Many grates are designed to be cut away in segments as the tree grows, but this is expensive.

TRUNK WRAPS

In northern climates, trunks of thin- and/or smooth-barked trees are wrapped to prevent injury from winter sun. Inner bark temperatures often rise well above freezing on sunny winter days. A rapid temperature drop at night to below freezing temperatures sometimes causes injury to the cambium. Visible damage appears several months later as dead bark that sloughs off in a long narrow strip (Figure 7-18), usually on the south or southwest sides (217).

Wrapping materials that minimize the temperature changes in the bark should be the most effective method of preventing sunscald injury. However, paper wrap provides no improvement over an unwrapped trunk (202,217), but continues to be the accepted standard, and users consider it to be effective in preventing sunscald (170).

Trunks should be wrapped from the bottom to the top so that the layers overlap and shed water. At the top, secure the wrap with light twine or weatherproof tape that will stretch slightly as the trunk grows. Never use nylon cord or fiber-reinforced tape.

Plastic guards are sometimes used as protection against damage from sun, equipment, and animals (Figure 7-19). These guards can prevent small mammals from feeding on the bark at the tree base that can girdle the stem. Guards protect against mechanical injury by lawn mowers and string trimmer weed whips, which can be a major problem for trees in the landscape. Thin barked trees and palms are most susceptible to damage. In trees stressed from transplanting, small wounds can enlarge to become a serious problem.

FIGURE 7-18. When sun warms the bark to above freezing in winter, or to very high temperatures in summer, damage can occur on newly planted, thin, smooth-barked trees. Planting a tree in a different orientation than it was in the nursery may increase susceptibility of some tree species to bark injury from sun exposure.

FIGURE 7-19. Trunks of small trees can be protected from mowers and string trimmers by a simple 6 in (15 cm) high piece of flexible plastic drain pipe, slit down the side to get it around the trunk. Animal protection may require a taller guard. The entire trunk is often covered on golf courses to protect young trees from golf balls.

MULCHING

Mulch can be used to conserve soil moisture, to buffer soil temperature extremes, to control weeds and other competing vegetation, and to replenish organic matter and nutrients in the soil. All of these effects lead to improved root growth in the soil beneath the mulch as well as in the well-established organic mulch layer itself (Figure 7-20). The roots in the mulch will not be at any greater risk of desiccation, since a well-established layer of mulch can hold more water than the soil itself, without decreasing aeration to the soil beneath it (206,239).

The majority of tree species used in the landscape evolved in a woodland environment and their root systems do not compete well against lawn grasses. In newly planted trees, mulching at the time of planting resulted in a 400 percent increase in fine root development in the top 6 in (15 cm) of soil, partially because grass competition is eliminated (197). Aboveground growth is also increased by mulching (Figure 7-21) (192,197,223,243,246). High levels of watering and fertilization can help to overcome grass competition, but not completely. In addition to competition for water and nutrients, some lawn grasses may be able to reduce the growth of the trees through chemicals they produce. This is called **allelopathy**. Fescues have been shown to stunt the growth of southern magnolia

FIGURE 7-20. Sugar maple (*Acer saccharum*) roots grow better under mulch than when in competition with grass.

FIGURE 7-21.   Mulched trees (as shown on the right) grow more vigorously than those without mulch (as shown on the left). (photo credit - T. Green)

(*Magnolia grandiflora*) (200), black walnut (*Juglans nigra*) (233), and sweetgum (*Liquidambar stryaciflua*) (238). Combinations of other trees and grasses have not been studied.

The size of the mulched area needed will depend somewhat on the size of the plant. For typical-size landscape trees (up to 3 in (8 cm) caliper), a 6-9 ft (2-3 m) diameter circle of mulch is best (Figure 7-22). This will cover the area where roots will grow during the first half of the establishment period (see Chapter 9). Trees will benefit longer from larger areas of mulch, but even a small circle of mulch around the trunk will reduce lawn mower injury. Mulch applied directly over turfgrass will usually smother it. Deep tilling the soil around the outside of the planting hole under the entire mulched area would be recommended to create a larger planting hole for better root growth. In northern climates it may be best not to apply mulch to plants installed in the early spring until after the soil has warmed because it may delay soil-warming (222). This is usually not as much of a problem with established mulch areas because the soil does not get as cold under the mulch during the winter.

Composted organic materials are best for mulch. Composting before use will eliminate potential nutrient imbalances, and may kill plant pathogens and increase microorganisms that suppress disease (207,208). Research has never shown that vascular diseases, such as Dutch elm disease and Verticillium wilt, can be transmitted in mulch, and it is not usually considered to be a problem in practice. However, it has not been proven to be absolutely safe either.

The mulch layer should be 2-4 in (5-10 cm) deep after settling. A layer any thinner will need replenishment too soon. A layer any thicker would be out of proportion to the size of most new plants, providing no additional benefits. The

FIGURE 7-22. Mulch an area 3 times the diameter of the root ball with 2-4 in (5-10 cm) of wood chips. The soil ring at the edge of the root ball will usually be visible through the mulch.

mulch should not be allowed to cover the base of the trunk. This could lead to bark injury from fungi or rodents. Mulch is often incorrectly piled up to 1 ft (30 cm) deep in a small circle only about 3 ft (1 m) wide around the tree. This is of little benefit to the roots, potentially damaging to the trunk, and aesthetically unpleasing.

Sheets of plastic or geotextile fabric are sometimes used under mulch to control weeds. Plastic can cause roots to grow at, or near, the soil surface, presumably because of reduced aeration in deeper soils (245). Weed shoots and roots can penetrate many of the fabrics. Decomposing mulch on top of the fabric or plastic creates an excellent environment for weeds to establish, though the fabric can reduce the time required for weeding the mulch (186). The geotextile fabric under mulch can sometimes become so clogged with gravel and debris that water and air cannot pass through. It also prevents the humus from the decomposing mulch from being incorporated into the soil.

FERTILIZERS AND ROOT STIMULANTS

It is difficult to make general recommendations about fertilizing after planting that would apply to all situations. Length of the establishment period, production method, fertilizer formulation, and maintenance after planting must all be considered.

Drought stress limits the growth of newly planted trees immediately after planting more than any other factor. Until the root system can grow and absorb more water, adding nutrients to the soil is likely to be ineffective (203,225,226,231,235,247).

There are many factors that determine how soon after planting that fertilizing will be effective. Small plants require less time to regenerate their root system and can overcome their water shortage problem more quickly than large plants. Plants with a constant and ample supply of soil moisture will be less water stressed, regenerate roots more quickly, and benefit from fertilization earlier than infrequently irrigated plants. If the soil-less media in container plant root balls has low nutrient-holding capacity, these plants may require earlier and more frequent fertilization to avoid nutrient deficiency until the roots grow out into the backfill and site soils. Very small plants that overcome post-planting stress very rapidly may benefit from slow-release fertilizer applied at planting.

Unless the soil is nutrient deficient, it is usually best to wait until a year or more after planting to fertilize. Rates from 3 to 6 lb of actual nitrogen per 1000 sq ft (1.5 to 3 kg/100 sq m) have been shown to increase growth of young trees (205,224,235,236). Avoid formulations with high salt indexes (Table 7-1), especially where a salt problem already exists, such as along streets where deicing salts are used.

Fertilization, especially with phosphorous, is often thought to cause a direct increase in root growth. There is no evidence that phosphorous will increase root growth unless the soil is phosphorous deficient. Nitrogen can cause a localized

TABLE 7-1. Salt indexes and nutrient content of common fertilizers.

Fertilizer	%N	%P_2O_5	%K_2O	Salt Index
Ammonium nitrate	35.0	-	-	104.7
Ammonium sulfate	21.2	-	-	69.0
Sodium nitrate	16.5	-	-	100.0
Potassium nitrate	13.8	-	-	73.6
Urea	46.6	-	-	75.4
Natural Organic	4.0	-	-	3.5
Monoammonium phosphate	12.2	-	-	29.9
Diammonium phosphate	21.2	-	-	34.2
Superphosphate	-	20.2	-	7.8
Triple superphosphate	-	48.0	-	10.0
Monoammonium phosphate	-	61.7	-	29.9
Diammonium phosphate	-	53.8	-	34.2
Monopotassium phosphate	-	52.2	-	8.4
Potassium chloride	-	-	60.0	116.3
Potassium nitrate	-	-	46.6	73.6
Potassium sulphate	-	-	54.0	46.1
Monopotassium phosphate	-	-	34.6	8.4

increase in root growth (184,240), but other parts of the root system may be reduced (244). Nitrogen may just alter the distribution of the fine roots. It is also thought that if fertilizer increases crown development, more carbohydrates will be translocated to the roots and increase root growth, but transplanted trees already have high levels of carbohydrates in the roots (242).

Many compounds have been marketed as root stimulants. Contents of these may include growth hormones, nutrients, vitamins, sugars, amino acids, humic acids, extracts of plants, and inoculum of beneficial rhizosphere fungi and bacteria. Very little research information from studies on landscape trees and shrubs has been published on these products, so it is not possible to know if they are actually beneficial when added at planting time.

ANTITRANSPIRANTS

Antitranspirants are foliage sprays that reduce water loss through the leaf surface (182,228). Several antitranspirants are available. These are essentially waxes, resins, and plastics. The spray dries and forms a thin protective film on the leaf surface that usually lasts for several weeks before it weathers off. If the leaves are growing when the spray is applied, the film cracks and eventually looses its effectiveness.

Certain film-antitranspirants may be detrimental to normal leaf respiration when used improperly (215), and they can reduce root and shoot growth (228). Film-forming antitranspirants are variably effective, depending upon the compound, the plant species, and environmental conditions. On some evergreens, such as pines, the compounds combine with the waxes in the stomatal pores and form impermeable plugs. These plugs reduce water loss but also reduce photosynthesis due to limited diffusion of CO_2. Some antitranspirants are toxic to certain species and non-toxic to others. In general, antitranspirants appear to be more toxic to evergreens than to deciduous species. Due to the reduction in cooling effect and water evaporation on the leaf surfaces, high air temperatures and bright sun may cause heat injury to leaves that have been sprayed.

Despite possible toxicity problems, antitranspirants provide a useful method of manipulating the water balance of plants after transplanting (185). They have been used in summer transplanting with success (198,210). When deciduous plants must be moved in leaf, the use of antitranspirants may be warranted in order to reduce the possibly that plants will reach the permanent wilting stage. In colder climates, evergreens may be protected from winter desiccation when a spray is applied in late fall. An additional application may be necessary during a mild period in mid-winter. **The use of antitranspirants should not be substituted for good transplanting practices.**

TREESHELTERS

Originally used to aid in establishment of seedlings in reforestation, treeshelters are sometimes used in nursery and landscape situations (181,229). Treeshelters are translucent tubes that are placed around small seedlings. The bottom of the tube must be in complete contact with the soil to protect the seedling from animal damage, and the unit is held in place by a stake (Figure 7-23). Air temperature, relative humidity, and carbon dioxide concentrations are higher inside the treeshelters, providing a greenhouse-like effect that often results in increased height growth (181,183,213,227) and survival (183,214).

Several studies have shown that treeshelters can decrease caliper growth in the first few seasons and the trunks of these trees may be incapable of supporting the weight of the top when the treeshelter is removed (179,180,213,232). The problem appears to be a result of the need to remove the treeshelter prematurely in landscape and nursery situations. Originally used in reforestation plantings, treeshelters were intended to be left in place for at least 5 years until weathering caused them to gradually deteriorate and fall away. A tree that looses support of the shelter gradually is able to develop trunk taper and stand upright on its own (227).

Treeshelters can reduce root development (180,181,232), but the reasons are unclear. If removal of the shelter resulted in increased transpiration, severe water stress could result from the smaller root system.

Treeshelters seem to be most beneficial when used for their original purpose — to aid in the establishment of seedlings in reforestation where they would remain in place until they deteriorate. Removing them prematurely and abruptly results in weak trunks. They seem to be most effective in cool, summer climates where both the greenhouse effect and rodent protection help to increase survival. They are ineffective in Mediterranean climates without irrigation (183).

FIGURE 7-23. Treeshelters can increase survival and shoot growth of seedlings by protecting them from animal damage and providing a greenhouse-like environment. Roots and trunks may grow slower when treeshelters are used. The effectiveness of treeshelters varies with climate.

FINAL INSPECTION

The final step in the planting process is inspection. There are many things that need to be checked:

- Is the planting depth correct?
- Is the trunk straight?
- Has a raised ring of soil been formed to hold irrigation water over the root ball?
- Does the pruning job look good from all directions?
- Has the plant been mulched without covering the base of the trunk?
- Was the plant watered thoroughly?
- Has the extra soil, root ball wrappings, pruned branches and other debris been removed from the site?
- If the plant needed staking, do the ties allow for growth and movement of the trunk?
- Does the new owner or maintenance crew understand how important proper care will be for the survival and good health of the new plant?

It might seem like the job is done once the new plant is in the ground and everything is cleaned up, but it is not. It may have taken weeks, or longer, to choose the right tree and plant it properly, but it may take years for the new plant to establish, especially larger trees. Throughout this period an ongoing commitment to maintenance will be required.

LITERATURE CITED

169. Anonymous 1995. Tree-Pruning Guidelines. International Society of Arboriculture, Savoy, Illinois. 14 pp.
170. Appleton, B.A. and S. French. 1992. *Current attitudes toward and uses of tree trunk protective wraps, paints and devices.* J. Arboric. 18:15-20.
171. Appleton, B.A. and C.E. Whitcomb. 1983. *Effects of container size and transplanting date on the growth of tree seedlings.* J. Environ. Hort. 1:89-93.
172. Arnold, M.A. 1996. *Mechanical correction and chemical avoidance of circling roots differentially affect post-transplant root regeneration and field establishment of container-grown Shumard oak.* J. Am. Soc. Hort. Sci. 121:258-263.
173. Askew, J.C., C.H. Gilliam, H.G. Ponder, and G.J. Kever. 1985. *Transplanting leafed-out bare root dogwood liners.* HortSci. 20:219-221.
174. Blessing, S.C. and M.N. Dana. 1987. *Post-transplant root system expansion in Juniperus chinensis L. and influenced by production system, mechanical root disruption and soil type.* J. Environ. Hort. 5:155-158.
175. Birdel, R., C. Whitcomb, and B.A. Appleton. 1983. *Planting techniques for tree spade dug trees.* J. Arboric. 9:282-284.
176. Broschat, T.K. 1991. *Effects of leaf removal on survival of transplanted Sabal palms.* J. Arboric. 17:32-33.
177. Broschat, T.K. 1994. *Effects of leaf removal, leaf tying, and overhead irrigation on transplanted pygmy date palms.* J. Arboric. 17:32-33.
178. Broschat, T. 1995. *Planting depth affects root growth and nutrient content of transplanted Pygmy date palms.* HortSci. 30:1031-1032.

179. Burger, D.W., G.W. Forister, and P.A. Kiehl. 1996. *Height, caliper growth, and biomass response of ten shade tree species to treeshelters.* J. Arboric. 22:161-166.

180. Burger, D.W., G.W. Forister, and R. Gross. 1997. *Short and long-term effects of tree shelters on the root and stem growth of ornamental trees.* J. Arboric. 23:49-56.

181. Burger, D.W., P. Svihra, and R. Harris. 1992. *Treeshelter use in producing container grown trees.* HortSci. 27:30-32.

182. Castle, W.S. 1983. *Antitranspirant and root and canopy pruning effects on mechanically transplanted eight-year-old* Murcott *citrus trees.* J. Am. Soc. Hort. Sci. 108:981-985.

183. Costello, L.R., A. Peters, and G.A. Giusti. 1996. *An evaluation of treeshelter effects on plant survival and growth in a Mediterranean climate.* J. Arboric. 22:1-9.

184. Coutts, M.P. and J.J. Philipson. 1976. *The influence of mineral nutrition on the root development of trees. I. The growth of Sitka spruce with divided root systems.* J. Expt. Bot. 27:1102-1111.

185. Davenport, D.C., P.E. Martin, and R.M. Hagan. 1972. *Antitranspirants for conservation of leaf water potential of transplanted citrus trees.* HortSci. 7:511-512.

186. Derr, J.F. and B.A. Appleton. 1989. *Weed control with landscape fabrics.* J. Environ. Hort. 7:129-133.

187. Drilias, M.J., J.E. Kuntz, and G.L. Worf. 1982. *Collar rot and basal canker of sugar maple.* J. Arboric. 8:29-33.

188. Ellyard, R.K. 1984. *Effect of root pruning at time of planting on subsequent root development of two species of eucalyptus.* J. Arboric. 10:241-216.

189. Evans, P. and J. Klett. 1984. *The effects of dormant pruning treatments on leaf, shoot and root production from bare-root* Malus sargentii. J. Arboric. 10:298-302.

190. Evans, P. and J. Klett. 1985. *The effects of dormant branch thinning on total leaf, shoot, and root production from bare-root* Prunus cerasifera Newportii. J. Arboric 11:149-151.

191. Fuecht, J.R. 1986. *Wire baskets can be slow killers of trees.* Am. Nurseryman 163:156-159.

192. Fraedrich, S.W. and D.L. Ham. 1982. *Woodchip mulching around maples: Effect on tree growth and soil characteristics.* J. Arboric. 8:85-89.

193. Gardner-Young, J.W. 1981. *A new method of planting trees and shrubs.* J. Arboric. 5:45-48.

194. Gilman, E.F. 1997. Trees for Urban and Suburban Landscapes: An Illustrated Guide to Pruning. Delman Publishers, Inc. Albany, NY. 172 pp.

195. Gilman, E.F., T.H. Yeager, and D. Weigle. 1996. *Fertilizer, irrigation and root ball slicing affects Burford holly growth after planting.* J. Environ. Hort. 14:105-110.

196. Goodwin, C. and G. Lumis. 1992. *Embedded wire in tree roots: Implications for tree growth and root function.* J. Arboric. 18:115-122.

197. Green, T.L., and G.W. Watson. 1989. *Effects of turfgrass and mulch on the establishment and growth of bare-root sugar maples.* J. Arboric. 15:268-272.

198. Harris, R.W. 1992. Arboriculture: Integrated Management of Landscape Trees, Shrubs and Vines. Prentice Hall, Englewood Cliffs, NJ. 674 pp.

199. Harris, J.R. and N.L. Bassuk. 1995. *Effects of defoliation and antitranspiration on transplant response of scarlet oak, green ash and Turkish hazelnut.* J. Arboric. 21:33-36.

200. Harris, R.W., J.L. Paul, and A.T. Leiser. 1977. Fertilizing woody plants. Univ. Calif. Agr. Sci. Leaflet No. #2576. 23 pp.

201. Harris, R.W., A.T. Leiser, and W.B. Davis. 1978. Staking landscape trees. University of California, Davis, Division of Agricultural Sciences Leaflet No. #2576. 13 pp.

202. Hart, J.H. and G.K. Dennis. 1978. *Effect of tree wrap on the incidence of frost cracks in Norway maple*. J. Arboric. 4:226-227.

203. Heisler, G.M., R.E. Schutzki, R.P. Zisa, H.G. Halverson, and B.A. Hamilton. 1982. *Effect of planting procedures on initial growth of* Acer rubrum *L. and* Fraxinus pennsylvanicum *L. in a parking lot*. USDA For. Serv. Res. Paper NE-513. 6 pp.

204. Hensley, D.L. and C.F. Fackler. 1984. *Do water-holding compounds help in transplanting?* Am. Nurseryman. 159:93.

205. Himelick, E.B., D. Neely, and W.R. Crowly, Jr. 1965. *Experimental field studies on shade tree fertilization*. Illinois Nat. Hist. Survey Biological Notes 53. 12 pp.

206. Himelick, E.B. and G.W. Watson. 1990. *Reduction of oak chlorosis with wood chip mulch treatments*. J. Arboric. 16:275-278.

207. Hoitink, H.A.J., A.G. Stone, and D.Y. Han. 1997. *Suppression of plant diseases by composts*. HortSci. 32:184-187.

208. Hoitink, H.A.J., D.M. VanDoren Jr., and A.F. Schitthenner. 1977. *Suppresssion of* Phytophthora cinnamomi *in a composted hardwood bark potting medium*. Phytopathology 67:561-565.

209. Holmes, F.W. 1984. *Effects of maples of prolonged exposure by artificial girdling roots*. J. Arboric. 10:40-44.

210. Hummel, R. 1990. *Water relations of container-grown woody and herbaceous plants following antitranspirant sprays*. HortSci. 25:772-775.

211. Hummel, R.L. and C.R. Johnson. 1986. *Influence of pruning at transplant time on growth and establishment of* Liquidambar styraciflua *L., sweet gum*. J. Am. Soc. Hort. Sci. 4:83-86.

212. Kielbaso, J.J. and J.H. Hart. 1996. Comparison of commercial compounds to promote wound closure on Michigan hardwoods. Abstract, Amer. Phytopath. Soc. Conf., Indianapolis, IN.

213. Kjelgren, R. 1994. *Growth and water relations of Kentucky coffee tree in protective shelters during establishment*. HortSci. 29:777-780.

214. Kjelgren, R., B. Cleveland, and M. Foutch. 1994. *Establishment of white oak seedlings with three post-plant handling methods on deep-tilled minesoil during reclamation*. J. Environ. Hort. 12:100-103.

215. Kozlowski, T.T. and W.J. Davies. 1975. *Control of water balance in transplanted trees*. J. Arboric. 1:1-10.

216. Kuhns, M. 1997. *Penetration of treated and untreated burlap by roots of balled-and-burlapped Norway maples*. J. Arboric. 23:1-7.

217. Litzow, M. and H. Pellet. 1983. *Materials for potential use in sunscald prevention*. J. Arboric. 9:35-38.

218. Lumis, G.P. 1990. *Wire baskets: A further look*. Am. Nurseryman (August):128-131.

219. Lumis, G.P. and S.A. Struger. 1988. *Root tissue development around wire-basket transplant containers*. HortSci. 23:401.

220. Maleike, R. and R.L. Hummel. 1992. *Planting landscape plants*. J. Arboric. 16:217-226.

221. McDougall, D.N. and R.A. Blanchette. 1996. *Polyethylene plastic wrap for tree wounds: a promoter of wound closure on fresh wounds*. J. Arboric. 22:206-210.

222. Myers, K. and H.C. Harrison. 1988. *Evaluation of container plantings in an urban environment*. J. Arboric. 14:293-297.

223. Neely, D. 1984. *Grass competition for nitrogen around landscape trees*. J. Environ. Hort. 2:86-87.

224. Neely, D., E.B. Himelick, and W.R. Crowley, Jr. 1970. Fertilization of Established Trees: A Report of Field Studies. Illinois Nat. Hist. Survey Bulletin No. #30: 235-266.

225. Perry, E. and G.W. Hickman. 1992. *Growth response of newly planted valley oak trees to supplemental fertilizers.* J. Environ. Hort. 10:242-244.

226. Ponder, H.G., C.H. Gilliam, E. Wilkenson, J. Eason, and C.E. Evans. 1984. *Influence of trickle irrigation and nitrogen rates to* Acer rubrum *L.* J. Environ. Hort. 2:40-43.

227. Potter, M.J. 1991. Treeshelters. Forestry Commission Handbook 7, HMSO, London.

228. Ranney, T.G., N.L. Bassuk, and T.H. Whitlow. 1989. *Effect of transplanting practices on growth and water relations of 'Colt' cherry trees during reestablishment.* J. Environ. Hort. 7:41-45.

229. Reichenbach, M.R. and J. Roush. 1991. *Trees please!* J. Arboric. 17:334.

230. Schnelle, M.A. and J.E. Klett. 1992. *The effects of cold storage and dormant pruning on growth of* radiant *crabapple.* J. Arboric. 18:136-143.

231. Shoup, S., R. Reavis, and C. Whitcomb. 1981. *Effects of pruning and fertilizers on establishment of bareroot deciduous trees.* J. Arboric. 7:155-157.

232. Svihra, P., D. Burger, and R. Harris. 1996. *Treeshelter effect on root development of redwood trees.* J. Arboric. 22:174-179.

233 Todhunter, M.N. and W.F. Beineke. 1979. *Effect of fescue on black walnut growth.* Tree Planters's Notes, (Summer): 20-23.

234. Toliver, J.R., R.C. Sparks, and T. Hansbrough. 1980. *Effects of top and lateral pruning on survival and early growth - three bottomland hardwood tree species.* Tree Plant. Notes 31:13-15.

235. van de Werken, H. 1980. *Fertilization and other factors enhancing the growth rate of young shade trees.* J. Arboric. 7:33-37.

236. van de Werken, H. 1984. *Fertilization practices as they influence the growth rate of young shade trees.* J. Environ. Hort. 2:64-69.

237. von der Heide-Spravka, K.G., and G.W. Watson. 1990. *Directional variation in growth of trees.* J. Arboric. 16:169-173.

238. Walters, D.T. and A.R. Gilmore. 1976. *Allelopathic effects of fescue on growth of sweetgum.* J. Chem. Ecol. 2:469-79.

239. Watson, G.W. 1988. *Organic mulch and grass competition influence tree root development.* J. Arboric. 14:200-203.

240. Watson, G.W. 1994. *Root growth response to fertilizers.* J. Arboric. 20:4-8.

241. Watson, G.W. and E.B. Himelick. 1982. *Root distribution of nursery trees and its relationship to transplanting success.* J. Arboric. 8:225-229.

242. Watson, G.W. and E.B. Himelick. 1982. *Seasonal variation in root regeneration of transplanted trees.* J. Arboric. 8:305-3310.

243. Welker, W.V. and D.M. Glenn. 1985. *The relationship of sod proximity to the growth and nutrient composition of newly planted peach trees.* HortSci. 20:417-418.

244. Weller, F. 1966. *Horizontal distribution of absorbing roots and the utilization of fertilizers in apple orchards.* Erwobstbsobstbau 8:181-184.

245. Whitcomb, C.E. 1980. *Effects of black plastic and mulches on growth and survival of landscape plants.* J. Arboric. 6:10-12.

246. Whitcomb, C.E. 1981. *Response of woody landscape plants to Bermuda grass competition and fertility.* J. Arboric 7:191-194.

247. Wright, R.D. and E.B. Hale. 1983. *Growth of three shade tree genera as influenced by irrigation and nitrogen rates.* J. Environ. Hort. 1:5-6.

Establishment

If the plant is to survive and thrive at its new site, rapid root proliferation into the backfill and then into the site soil is imperative. The plant must not only dramatically increase its absorptive root surface area to gain access to a greater reservoir of soil moisture, it must often do so while coping with poor quality soils and limited root space.

How long it takes a tree to become established in the landscape depends on many factors; some of them can be controlled and some cannot. Tree establishment depends on the species, size of the tree, site conditions, care, and even climate. Understanding how long a tree will require a high level maintenance, and your ability to provide it, may influence your selection of tree size and species.

The level of horticultural care is usually different in the landscape than it was in the nursery where plants are grown in large uniform blocks with closely monitored irrigation, fertility, and pest control. In the landscape, there are often a wide variety of plants in a small space. Requirements of each plant vary, as do the environmental conditions on the site.

Even the most skilled and well-intentioned horticulturist will have difficulty providing optimum care constantly for every individual plant. Water stress that is overlooked for just a short time can seriously reduce root regeneration and delay establishment.

chapter

8

Root Development After Planting

Root systems normally spread far beyond the branch tips (Figure 8-1). In this large soil volume, much water is available to the roots. When field-grown plants are harvested, most of the root system remains in the nursery. Even though root loss of container plants is minimal, the roots are confined to the small volume of container soil. This soil can become excessively dry when moved to the landscape. The problem for both container and field-grown plants is the same: marginal or insufficient water absorption by the root system. The resulting water stress is a common cause of planting failure.

Until there is new root growth to develop a normal, spreading root system, the plant's survival in the landscape is very tenuous. Rapid root growth at the new site can occur only if all the requirements for root growth are sufficiently available. Understanding the process of root regeneration is probably one of the most important subjects related to successful tree and shrub planting.

ROOT DISTRIBUTION

In a root survey of 4,000 trees blown down by hurricane winds in England (257), root systems were categorized into root types using a system similar to that previously described by Wilde (309) (Figure 8-2). Major roots growing horizontally near the soil surface characterize lateral root (or plateroot) systems. These were the predominant types, 82.5 percent of all trees reported (Figure 8-2 right). Sloping root (or heartroot) systems have roots growing at many angles between horizontal and vertical (Figure 8-2 center). Fifteen percent of the trees had this

137

FIGURE 8-1. The large lateral roots forming the root flare often grow very horizontally, just a few inches below the surface, and can extend great distances. After tapering noticeably within a few feet of the trunk, the root becomes more rope-like, tapering very slowly.

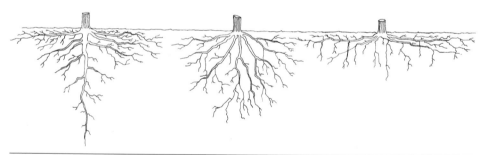

FIGURE 8-2. The basic root structure types; taproot, often with large laterals also (left), sloping or heartroot (center), lateral or plateroot (right).

type of root structure. Trees with true taproots also had substantial lateral roots, and occurred on only 2.5 percent of all trees (Figure 8-2 left).

In the nursery growing field, a typical landscape-sized tree (2-4 in (5-10 cm) caliper), will have a root system dominated by laterals that spread two to three times as wide as the branches spread (Figure 8-3). Branch roots develop over the entire length of these major lateral roots, dividing repeatedly and terminating as fine roots. The development of numerous branch roots on all lateral roots, and constant replacement of fine roots on these branch roots, results in the presence of fine absorbing roots virtually everywhere in the top few inches of surface soil. Strong taproots will be limited to a few species, such as oaks (*Quercus*) and walnut (*Juglans*), and usually to plants never transplanted in the nursery.

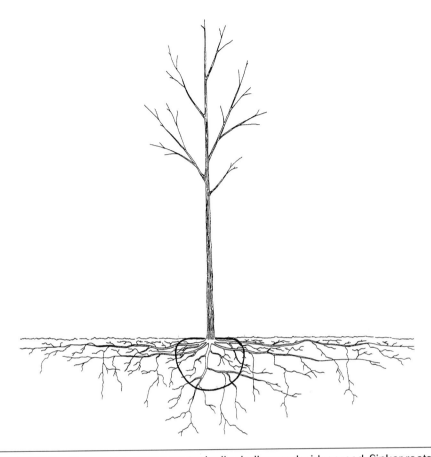

FIGURE 8-3.   Tree root systems are typically shallow and widespread. Sinker roots can follow natural openings into deeper soils. Tap roots are rare. Fine roots are present near the soil surface throughout the entire root system. Only a small percentage of the roots of field-grown trees are moved with the tree.

Palm trees are not woody plants and are anatomically similar to grasses, lilies, bamboos, and orchids. Root systems of palm species usually consist of numerous closely spaced and rather small, tube-like roots that radiate out from the base of the trunk with little or no branching (Figure 8-4).

ROOT LOSS

Digging

Bare root plants may loose nearly all of their fine roots during transplanting. Many are broken off as they are dug from the soil. Fine roots are very short lived under the best of conditions. The mechanical damage and desiccation caused by transplanting further reduce their longevity. Though fine root loss is severe on bare root plants, a large percentage woody roots are moved with the plant. New fine roots can redevelop rapidly under favorable conditions (Figure 8-5).

FIGURE 8-4. Tube-like roots of a palm tree. (photo credit - E. Gilman)

FIGURE 8-5. The root system of a bare root tree as it is shipped from nursery. Many of the fine roots may not survive, but they will soon be replaced by new fine roots from the many woody roots.

Root balls of field-grown trees, dug according to American Association of Nurserymen standards (248), contain less than 5-18 percent of the fine absorbing roots (261,263,308). Species that are difficult-to-transplant characteristically have fewer small diameter roots in the root ball than species that are easy-to-transplant (259,269,298). Trees grown in nurseries using trickle irrigation and root pruning practices have more roots in the root ball than trees from unmanaged plantations or from the wild (264).

Unless the outer portion of the root ball is sliced to eliminate circling roots, container plants suffer no substantial root loss during the planting process.

Nevertheless, container plants also experience post-planting stress (268). The specialized container media may retain water poorly in the landscape (293), and the plants are often approaching maximum allowable size for the container at time of sale.

Roots are good compartmentalizers (292). They are subject to frequent wounding by elements of their environment, such as burrowing animals and natural movement of the soil from freeze/thaw and wet/dry cycles. This wounding takes place in the presence of decay-causing organisms that are always present in the soil. Even the process of lateral and adventitious root formation causes a wound. **Response to natural wounding in the environment has lead to excellent compartmentalization (walling off decay to limit its spread) in roots.** Individual plants that are not good compartmentalizers will perform poorly during propagation and early stages of production when much wounding occurs. Poor compartmentalizers are not likely to reach the landscape. There is little need to worry that transplanting will introduce serious wood decay through the roots severed. Poor management, especially overwatering, can increase some root diseases, such as *Phytophthora*, on all plants, including transplants.

There is concern that vascular fungi such as *Verticillium* can enter severed roots of susceptible plants and infect and kill plants after transplanting. Verticillium wilt potentially can be a serious vascular disease. If the fungus is present in the soil it may infect new plantings. Root wounds caused by transplanting can increase the probability of infection by a vascular disease. *Verticillium* is a soil-borne fungus and can be transported to a new site in the soil ball or any soil adhering to bare root plants. Infested nursery soil known to have had *Verticillium* infected plants should not be transported to other sites to avoid the risk of introducing the *Verticillium* fungus to other sites.

Shipping

Transporting nursery stock can cause additional root damage, mostly from desiccation and mechanical damage. Excessive drying of the soil ball can be a serious problem, especially if the plants are in leaf. The outer few inches of a small soil ball can contain 50 percent of the total soil volume. When this outer layer of soil is allowed to dry out, half of the fine roots can be damaged. Once the soil ball dries, it can be very difficult to rewet thoroughly.

Mechanical damage is not uncommon during transport and handling. Even the most careful handling can sometimes result in cracking or distorting the root ball, especially if the soil is too dry or too wet. A long ride on a truck bed can flatten the root ball. When the soil shifts within the root ball, fine roots are torn or broken. If the root ball is dropped, or roughly handled, major root damage can result. Roots of bare root plants are also easily broken. Plants in containers are more resistant to root damage during shipping.

Storage

Sensitivity to desiccation during handling and storage is mainly responsible for poor root regrowth of bare-rooted plants. Moderate water stress can reduce root regeneration; high water stress can stop root regeneration (300). Sub-zero storage temperatures reduce the rate of respiration and disease incidence, but induce high moisture stress. The optimum storage temperature for most trees and shrubs is just above freezing (256).

Field-grown ball and burlap plants are best dug in late winter or early spring while they are still dormant, but are sometimes held for planting until later in the season. The holding area in the nursery yard should be well protected from the elements and irrigated. Root balls may be well covered with mulch, or sometimes they are temporarily replanted in holes lined with geotextile fabric until sold. Under these conditions, plants can be held for long periods without root damage. However, after plants are transported to the job site, storage conditions are rarely as favorable. A short delay of just two or three days before planting can result in serious drought stress in any type of planting stock. The root ball can heat up and roots will be killed if plants are stored in the hot sun. Soil temperatures in containers exposed to sun have been reported at more than 111°F (45°C) (253,260,276,281,284).

NEW ROOT GROWTH

The commonly used term, root regeneration, is most correctly applied to true transplanting situations where roots of balled and burlap and bare root stock are severed and must be replaced. Though roots are not "regenerated" on container plants, new root growth is just as important. Container plants must also develop roots that spread throughout a large volume of soil on the new site in order to have access to sufficient moisture. When the root system is confined to a small soil volume in a root ball or container soil, the available moisture will be removed by the plant **much** more rapidly than water can move from the surrounding soil to replace it. **The root ball can become dry enough to cause drought stress between rainfall and irrigation cycles, even though the surrounding soil may have ample moisture.** Cyclical drought stress is reduced by the development of a spreading root system in contact with a large volume of moisture containing soil.

When roots of field grown plants are severed at the perimeter of the root ball, nearly all new roots are produced near the end of the severed roots. Numerous new roots are initiated as a result of the wounding (307) (Figure 8-6). Contrary to traditional beliefs, very little new root initiation occurs between the cut ends and the base of the trunk.

When a root is severed, new roots formed at the cut surface will grow in the same direction as the original root. New roots forming slightly behind the cut surface grow out at more perpendicular angles to the original root (274).

The rate of root initiation (formation of a new roots) is affected by many factors, but under favorable experimental conditions, new roots are initiated after 17-29 days on green ash (*Fraxinus pennsylvanica*), which is considered an easy-to-transplant species (249). On red oak (*Quercus rubra*), a more difficult-to-transplant species, new root initiation did not take place for 24-49 days (295). In cool spring soils, a longer time would be required for new root initiation than in the warm soil conditions of this experiment. When trees are planted in the late fall, after soils have cooled, substantial new root growth may not occur until the

FIGURE 8-6.   When roots are severed during transplanting, nearly all of the new roots are produced near the cut end.

soils have warmed again in the spring. In warmer regions, active root growth may continue all winter if soils are warm. Mulch can help to keep soils warmer in winter.

Root extension rate (increase in length) depends on species and a number of environmental factors. Annual soil temperature regime is important. In the upper Midwestern United States (Hardiness zone 4-5), with its moderate summers and frozen soils in winter, roots grow at an average rate of 18 in (0.5 m) per year (301). Of course, for some species in certain soils, the rate of growth will be higher or lower, but this figure is a good average. In the subtropical climate of north central Florida (Hardiness zone 9) where light sandy soils predominate and the growing season is nearly year-round, root growth is more rapid—up to 6 ft (2 m) or more per year for some oak and citrus species that have been studied (255,262). Data for other climates are not available, but it should be possible to estimate. In general, it will take more than one season to replace the root system unless the plant is very small, or the growing season is very long.

Palms

It is commonly believed that if the tube-like roots of palms are cut during the digging process, they will usually die back, and new roots will originate from the root initiation zone at the base of the trunk. Actually, regrowth response of severed palm roots varies with species and distance from the base of the trunk (254). Less than 1 percent of all cut cabbage palm (*Sabal palmetto*) roots regenerated root tips, whereas coconut palms (*Cocos nucifera*) regenerated root tips about 50 percent of the time regardless of root stub length. Queen (*Syagrus romanzoffianum*) and royal palms (*Roystonea* sp.) regenerated more new root tips as length of the root stub was increased. Root pruning stimulated new roots from the root initiation zone for all species, but at a rate inversely proportional to the ability of the species to regenerate root tips on severed roots.

ENVIRONMENTAL FACTORS INFLUENCING ROOT GROWTH

Like most aspects of plant growth, the rate at which roots grow is influenced by numerous factors. Maximum daily root growth increments range from just a few millimeters in some species to over 56 mm in black locust (*Robinia pseudoacacia*), though average daily growth is usually much less (279).

Temperature

Most authors agree that root growth starts just before shoot growth in the spring, though considerable variation among species has been reported. Roots are often able to grow at lower temperatures than shoots (*i.e.* 41°F (5°C) for roots, 50°F(10°C) for shoots of sugar maple (*Acer saccharum*)). Roots are not dependent on shoots as a source of auxins (279,291). Maximal root growth in most tree species occurs in early summer. Optimum temperatures for root growth have been reported at 65°-89°F (18°-32°C), depending on species, with maximum temperatures for active growth reported at 77°-100°F (25°-38°C) (266,280,289,310). Roots of most woody species are killed at 104°-122°F (40°-50°C) (310). Root growth can be interrupted in midsummer due to unfavorable environmental conditions (drought or high temperature) with a second, but smaller period, of active growth in the late summer or early autumn when soil moisture and temperature again become more favorable. In temperate climates, root growth slows in the autumn as the soil cools and plants enter dormancy. Reported minimum temperatures for root growth range from 35°-52°F (2°-11°C) (279). Substantial root growth can continue throughout the winter in areas with mild winter temperatures. Roots can continue to grow in all non-frozen soil, but the rate will be reduced by cold soil temperatures. Root tissues of woody plants can be killed at soil temperatures of +23° to -4°F (-5° to -20°C) (272,284,294). Santamour (290) reported that all green ash roots from all provenances (origins) were killed at 4°F (-15°C).

Moisture

As soil begins to dry, development of branch roots is inhibited, but growth of primary roots is not (311). Root growth stops in most species when soil moisture is reduced to 12-14 percent (279) on an oven-dry basis, or -500 mbar soil moisture tension (251). Root suberization (the deposition of a waterproof layer in the walls of cells near the root surface) is accelerated in dry soil. As the effective absorbing surface is diminished, the roots do not regain their full capacity for water uptake until new root tips can be produced. When plants are rewatered immediately after cessation of root elongation, roots may not resume elongation for at least one week. Resumption of root growth takes up to five weeks if water is withheld longer (252). If the soil becomes too dry, some of the smaller roots may die.

An increase in moisture content above 40 percent induces almost no additional root growth. Roots are generally not sensitive to soil saturation itself, but secondary effects do have an impact on root growth. Wet soils are apt to be colder and reduce root growth. Excessive soil moisture reduces soil aeration because the water replaces the air normally held in the pores of the soil.

Aeration

Limited oxygen availability in saturated soils does have a substantial effect on the roots of most species. In most soils, 8 to 10 percent oxygen in the soil atmosphere is considered the minimum for good root growth. Below this level growth is inhibited. Roots may die if conditions become anaerobic. Roots of some species have lower oxygen requirements (285). When roots are deprived of adequate oxygen, leaf growth rate can be reduced (282). Lack of adequate gas exchange in waterlogged soils can also lead to an increase in carbon dioxide which is toxic to roots in higher than normal concentrations. In some plants, such as willow (*Salix*), alder (*Alnus*), poplar (*Populus*), tupelo (*Nyssa*), ash (*Fraxinus*), baldcypress (*Taxodium*), and birch (*Betula*), oxygen can move down to the roots internally through intercellular spaces. Enough oxygen can be transported so that some is released into the soil immediately surrounding the roots (273,277). This oxygen-transporting tissue within roots is called aerenchyma.

Soil density

Roots tend to follow the path of least resistance. Old root channels, animal tunnels, pockets of loose soil, cracks and fissures are often used by roots to penetrate the deeper, denser soils. Species with high root-to-shoot ratios seem to have a greater ability to penetrate hard soil layers. Compacted soils with high penetration resistance will slow the growth of roots. Bulk densities of 1.25-1.6 g/cc of soil will inhibit root growth (271,283,313). Soil strength (penetration resistance) may be more important than bulk density (299). Adequate soil moisture reduces penetration resistance.

Stored energy

Carbohydrates are often assumed to be in short supply in transplanted trees on the basis that much of the storage capacity (woody root tissue) is removed. Total carbohydrates stored in the root system may not be substantially reduced since many of the large roots (80 percent of total root weight) are contained in the root ball (264). Levels of stored carbohydrates (amount of carbohydrate per gram of root tissue) may be higher in transplanted trees one year after planting than in trees that are not moved (307). Though vigorous root growth from severed roots can require much energy, total root growth from the limited transplanted root system is probably less than that which would normally take place just to produce new root tips each year if the plant had a full root system. The amount of carbohydrates produced by the crown and stored in the transplanted root system is probably adequate to support this reduced level of growth.

Fertility

Concentrations of fine roots are often encountered in nutrient rich zones of soil (270,286,305). In nutrient rich soils, the growth of the main root is reduced and development of lateral roots is increased. This results in dense fine root development in these areas. Conversely, nutrient poor soils stimulate long roots with poorly developed laterals ("pioneer" roots). High nitrogen can stimulate top growth more than root growth, decreasing the root-shoot ratio (267). Heavy nitrogen fertilization at planting could be counter productive, reducing root extension and stimulating too much top growth. Contrary to traditional beliefs, phosphorous has not been shown to increase root growth of woody plants unless it is deficient in the soil (271,305,312).

REDEVELOPMENT OF ROOT STRUCTURE

Many new roots are formed at the cut end of a single root, but the stronger roots soon begin to dominate (274,296,302). The weaker roots persist only a short time (Figure 8-7). On Colorado spruce, a species with strong aboveground apical dominance, only a single regenerated root may persist on each severed root after about 5 years (Figure 8-8, left). Just a slight swelling and a few traces of the small

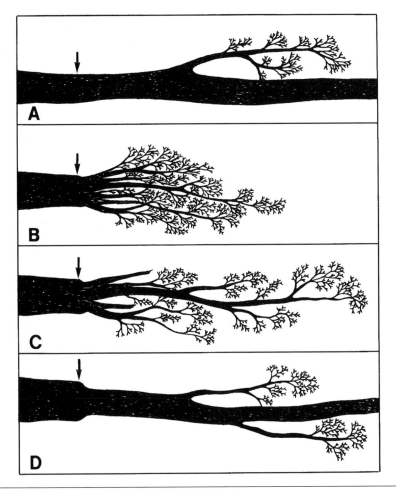

FIGURE 8-7.   Stages in replacement of a severed root. Root is severed at the arrow (A). Initially, many small roots are regenerated from the callus collar at the severed end (B). One root becomes dominant and continues to grow rapidly, while others stop growing or die (C). Eventually, only a single root may remain to replace the original root (D).

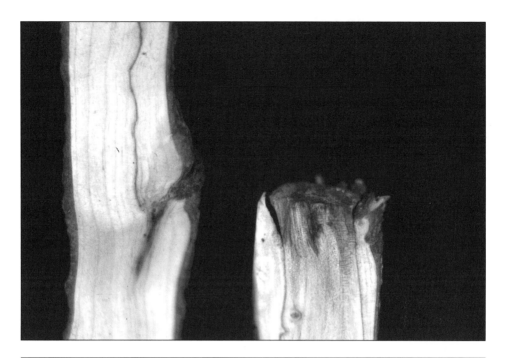

FIGURE 8-8.   When a spruce root more than a few millimeters in diameter is cut (right), a few small short-lived roots are regenerated but they soon disappear leaving only a "stub". When a small one or two year old is cut (left), the strongest regenerated root(s) usually dominate and become part of the new root structure, leaving little evidence that the other regenerated roots once were present (left). There is very little discoloration and decay resulting from the cuts.

dead roots are the only indication on the outside of the root that it was ever severed. On most maple species, which do not exhibit strong apical dominance aboveground, several regenerated roots may persist. Horsley et al. (275) cites evidence for apical dominance in roots, but further studies into the mechanism and significance of this pattern are needed.

Large severed roots are often quite visible at the surface of the root ball, and there is often great focus on damage to these root ends. What is often not appreciated is that much smaller and less visible roots also regenerate many new roots. Being smaller these roots are more subject to damage from desiccation if the exterior of the root ball dries out. In at least some species, all roots regenerated from the large severed roots may be gone after a few years, leaving only a "stub." On some of the very small one or two-year-old severed roots, several new roots are initiated after severing, with one eventually persisting and dominating. These roots continue to grow and develop into the new root system structure (Figure 8-8).

The root structure of landscape trees may be quite different than the root structure of naturally regenerated trees. Nursery-grown trees are sometimes transplanted several times during production. Each time roots are cut and new roots are regenerated. When the taproot is cut, growth of lateral roots near the surface increases and dependence on the taproot diminishes. Severing the taproot is necessary for transplanting, but might reduce the tree's ability to access deeper soil moisture, increasing the importance of proper care after transplanting. Rooted cuttings usually develop an entirely different initial root structure than those germinated from seed.

When roots of bare root plants are not spread out properly at planting, permanently kinked and twisted roots can result (Figure 8-9). Also, proper root development and anchorage will not occur, and vascular flow may be restricted.

Girdling roots (Figure 8-10) of field-grown stock (different than circling roots on container stock) can be formed as a result of transplanting (306). When primary roots (radially oriented lateral roots like spokes of a wheel) are severed by transplanting, existing branch roots often begin to grow more rapidly. Under normal circumstances, these branch roots would have remained small and probably live only a few years, before being replaced by other roots. But after the primary root is cut, they do sometimes become a part of the permanent structural root system. Their perpendicular orientation to the other major roots, and proximity to the base of the trunk, results in development of girdling roots as both the roots and the trunk continue to increase in diameter (Figure 8-11). These girdling roots restrict the flow in the vascular system and can cause stress, and eventually death of the tree. Additional evidence that girdling roots may result from transplanting is provided by the low incidence of girdling roots in nature.

FIGURE 8-9.   If the roots of bare root plants are not properly spread out at planting, a distorted root system will develop, sometimes referred to as a club foot.

FIGURE 8-10.   Girdling roots can be a problem because they restrict the flow of water and nutrients between the root system and the crown.

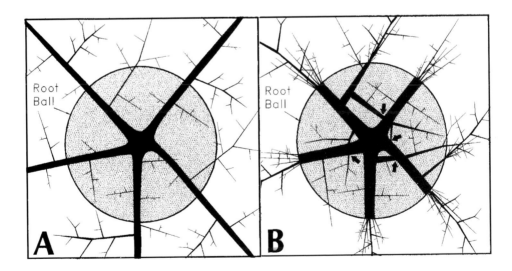

FIGURE 8-11.   Probable mechanism of girdling root formation. A. The major roots of a tree normally extend out from the trunk like spokes of a wheel. These roots and some of their branch roots, are severed during transplanting. B. After transplanting, new roots initiated near the cut ends grow in the direction of the original root, but growth of existing branch roots is stimulated and these can become girdling roots (arrows).

INCREASING ROOT GROWTH AFTER PLANTING

Traditional interest in root growth after planting has centered on the quantity of new roots produced by the newly planted tree or shrub. Growers strive for a dense development of fine roots on the basis that it is important for plant survival and new root growth after planting.

Root pruning in the nursery can increase the amount of fine root surface area in the root ball by 400 to 600 percent (265,308), but the percentage of the total root system length and surface area moved with the tree is still less than 18 percent (263,308). Root pruning may not always lead to better plant growth after transplanting (250,304).

In-ground fabric bags are designed to increase branching of the root system within a smaller root ball. The smaller soil volume in a smaller root ball will hold less water. This water will be depleted more rapidly than from a larger root ball, and water from the surrounding soil will not be able to move into the root ball as fast as it is absorbed by the roots. Increased root absorbing area in the root ball soil would have to be coupled with an ample supply of water in order to meet the soil moisture needs of the plant (288,304).

Auxin treatments can increase the number of new roots initiated near the cut ends. Indole-3-butyric acid (IBA) applied to roots near the edge of the root ball resulted in more root initiation (278,287,297), but may reduce root elongation (297). Napthaleneacidic acid (NAA) applied as a soil drench after planting also increased root initiation within a few centimeters of the severed root end in linden (*Tilia*) (303) (Figure 8-12). Gibberellin inhibiting growth regulators, such as paclobutrazol, may also promote root initiation (258).

Many kinds of root stimulating products have been marketed over the years. Claims usually refer to "better" or "improved" root growth without reference to specific effects on the root system or how they lead into faster establishment after planting. Ingredients range from vitamin compounds to seaweed extracts and growth hormones. The effectiveness of many of these products in stimulating root growth has not been shown convincingly in landscape situations through published independent studies. Use caution when judging unsubstantiated claims. If testing the products on your own, be sure to include untreated plants for a comparison (similar to the untreated control in a scientific experiment) to judge whether they are really effective.

Rapid root growth is important to minimize water stress after planting, but what kind of root growth should be promoted? Does a plant benefit from roots that are denser than would be found in the natural state? Will the extra roots remove water from the soil more quickly? If so, will water be absorbed so quickly from the small root zone that the plant will be subjected to more severe drought stress between watering cycles? Has the plant wasted the energy producing the extra roots? It would be better to encourage roots to elongate and to extend out into a larger soil volume as quickly as possible, rather than to produce more dense root development in a limited soil volume within and near the root ball. A large planting hole or a large area of cultivated soil around the root ball will help roots to spread out quickly, as will good care after planting.

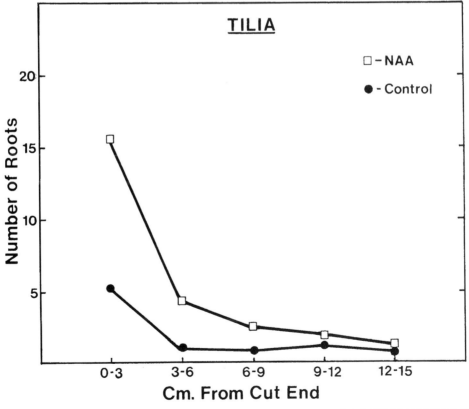

FIGURE 8-12.   The above photo is a root treated with NAA. Application of auxins to the cut root surface can increase root initiation near the severed end. The data proves what can be readily observed.

LITERATURE CITED

248. Anonymous. 1996. American Standard for Nursery Stock. ANSI Z60.1. American Association of Nurserymen, Washington, DC. 52 pp.

249. Arnold, M.A., and D.K. Struve. 1989. *Green ash establishment following transplant.* J. Am. Soc. Hort. Sci. 114:591-595.

250. Beeson Jr., R.C. 1994. *Water Relations of field-grown* Quercus virginiana *mill. from preharvest through containerization and 1 year into a landscape.* J. Am. Soc. Hort. Sci. 119:169-174.

251. Bevington, K.B. and W.S. Castle. 1985. *Annual root growth pattern of young citrus trees in relation to shoot growth, soil temperature and soil water.* J. Am. Soc. Hort. Sci. 110:840-845.

252. Bilan, M. 1974. Relationship between needle moisture and root growth in loblolly pine seedlings, pp. 219-221, **In** Hoffman, G. (Ed.). Ecology and Physiology of Root Growth. Academic-Verlag, Berlin.

253. Brass, T.J., G.J. Keever, C.H. Gilliam, and J. Eakes. 1996. *Styrene lining and container size affect substrate temperature.* J. Environ. Hort 14:184-186.

254. Broschat, T.K. and H.M. Donselman. 1984. *Regrowth of severed palm roots.* J. Arboric. 1:238-240.

255. Castle, W.S. 1983. *Antitranspirant and root canopy pruning effects on mechanically transplanted eight-year-old* Murcott *citrus trees.* J. Am. Soc. Hort. Sci. 108:981-985.

256. Cleary, B. and R. Tinus. 1980. *Preservation of nursery stock quality through packaging storage, transport and planting.* N.Z. J. of For. Sci. 10:295-296.

257. Cutler, D.F., P.E. Gasson, and M.C. Farmer. 1990. *The wind blown tree survey: analysis of results.* Arboricultural J. 14:265-286.

258. Davis, T.D., N. Sankhla, R.H. Walser, and A. Upadhyaya. 1985. *Promotion of adventitious root formation on cuttings by paclobutrazol.* HortSci. 20:883-885.

259. Fare, D.C., C.H. Gilliam, and H.G. Ponder. 1985. *Root distribution of two field-grown* Ilex. HortSci. 20:1129-1130.

260. Fretz, T.A. 1971. *Influence of physical conditions on summer temperatures in nursery containers.* HortSci. 6:400-401.

261. Gilman, E.F. 1988. *Tree root spread in relation to branch dripline and harvestable root ball.* HortSci. 23:351-353.

262. Gilman, E.F. and R.C. Beeson. 1996. *Production method affects tree establishment in the landscape.* J. Environ. Hort. 14:81-87.

263. Gilman, E.F. and R.C. Beeson. 1996. *Nursery production method affects root growth.* J. Environ. Hort. 14:88-91.

264. Gilman, E.R., R.C. Beeson Jr., and R.J. Black. 1992. *Comparing root balls on laurel oak transplanted from the wild with those of nursery and container grown trees.* J. Aboric. 18: 124-129.

265. Gilman, E.F. and T.H. Yeager. 1987. *Root pruning* Quercus virginiana *to promote a compact root system.* Proc. S. Nurs. Assoc. Res. Conf. 32:340-342.

266. Graves, R.G. 1994. *Urban soil temperatures and their potential impact on tree growth.* J.Arboric. 20:24-27.

267. Hamilton, D.F., M.E.C. Graca, and S.D. Verkade. 1981. *Critical effects of fertility on root and shoot growth of selected landscape plants.* J. Arboric. 7:281-290.

268. Harris, J.R. and E.F. Gilman. 1993. *Production method affects growth and post-transplant establishment of* East Palatka *holly.* J. Amer. Soc. Hort. Sci. 118:194-200.

269. Harris, J.R. and N.L. Bassuk. 1994. *Seasonal effects on transplantability of scarlet oak, green ash, Turkish hazelnut and tree lilac.* J. Arboric. 20:310-316.

270. Harris, R.W. 1992. *Root-shoot ratios.* J. Arboric. 18:39-41.

271. Harris, R.W. 1992. Arboriculture: Integrated Management of Landscape Trees, Shrubs and Vines. Prentice Hall, Englewood Cliffs, NJ. 674 pp.

272. Havis, J.R. 1976. *Root hardiness of woody ornamentals.* HortSci. 11:385-386.

273. Hook, D.D., C.L. Brown, and R.H. Wetmore. 1972. *Aeration in trees.* Botanical Gazette 133:443-454.

274. Horsley, S.B. 1971. *Root tip injury and development of the paper birch root system.* For. Sci. 17: 341-348.

275. Horsley, S.B. and B.F. Wilson. 1971. *Development of the woody portion of the root system of* Betula papyrifera. Amer. J. Bot. 58:141-147.

276. Ingram, D.L. 1981. *Characterization of temperature fluctuations and woody plant growth in white poly bags and conventional black containers.* HortSci. 16:762-763.

277. Kawase, M. 1981. *Anatomical and morphological adaptation of plants to waterlogging.* HortSci. 16:30-34.

278. Lumis, G.P. 1982. *Stimulating root regeneration of landscape-size red oak with auxin root sprays.* J. Arboric. 8:325-326.

279. Lyr, H. and G. Hoffmann. 1967. Growth rates and growth periodicity of tree roots, pp. 181-237, **In** Ronberger, J.A. and P. Mikola (Eds.). International Review of Forestry Research, Vol. 2. Academic Press, New York.

280. Martin, C.A. and D.L. Ingram. 1991. *Root growth of southern magnolia following exposure to high root-zone temperatures.* HortSci. 26:370-371.

281. Martin, C.A. and D.L. Ingram. 1993. *Container pattern dimension affects rooting medium temperature.* HortSci. 28:18-19.

282. Neuman, D.S. 1993. *Shoot responses to root stress - A resource gathering point of view.* J. Arboric. 19:118-123.

283. Oddiraju, V.G. and C.A. Beyl. 1996. *Root growth of seedlings and microcuttings of western black cherry grown in compacted soil.* HortSci. 31:453-457.

284. Pellett, H. 1981. *Soil temperature effects on urban plants.* New Horizons pp. 34-36.

285. Pezeshki, S.R. 1991. *Root responses of flood-tolerant and flood-sensitive tree species to soil redox conditions.* Trees 5:180-186.

286. Pham, C.H., H.G. Halverson, and G.M. Heisler. 1978. Red maple (*Acer rubrum* L.) growth and foliar nutrient responses to soil fertility level and water regime. USDA For. Ser. Res. Pap. NE-412.

287. Prager, C.M. and G.P. Lumis. 1983. *IBA and some IBA-synergist increases of root regeneration of landscape-sized trees.* J. Arboric. 9:117-123.

288. Reiger, R. and C. Whitcomb. 1985. *A root control system for growing and transplanting trees.* Arboric. J. 9:33-38.

289. Rohsler, M. 1982. *Root hardiness ratings of woody nursery plants.* Tennessee Nursery Digest Vol. 4, no. 5.: 2 pp.

290. Santamour Jr., F.S. 1979. *Root hardiness of green ash seedlings from different provenances.* J. Arboric. 5:276-278.

291. Scott T.K. 1972. *Auxins and roots.* Ann. Rev. Plant Physiol. 23:235-58.

292. Shigo, A.L. 1993. 100 Tree Myths. Shigo and Tree, Associates. Durham, NH. 80 pp.

293. Spomer, L.A. 1980. *Container soil water relations: production, maintenance, and transplanting.* J. Arboric. 6:315-320.

294. Studer, E.J., P.L. Steponkus, G.L. Good, and S.L. Wiest. 1978. *Root hardiness of container-grown ornamentals.* HortSci. 13:172-174.

295. Struve, D.K. 1990. *Root regeneration in transplanted deciduous nursery stock.* HortSci. 25:266-270.

296. Struve, D.K. and F.A. Blazich. 1982. *Comparison of three methods of auxin application on rooting of eastern white pine stem cuttings.* For. Sci. 28:337-344.

297. Struve, D.K. and B.C. Moser. 1984. *Auxin effects on root regeneration of scarlet oak seedlings.* J. Am. Soc. Hort. Sci. 109:91-95.

298. Struve, D.K. and B.C. Moser. 1984. *Root system and root regeneration characteristics of pin and scarlet oak.* HortSci. 19:123-125.

299. Taylor, H.M. and H.R. Gardner. 1963. *Penetration of cotton seedling taproots as influenced by bulk density, moisture content, and strength of soil.* Soil Sci. 96:153-156.

300. Tinus, R.W. 1996. *Root growth potential as an indicator of drought stress history.* Tree Physiol. 16:795-799.

301. Watson, G. 1985. *Tree size affects root regeneration and top growth after transplanting.* J. Arboric. 11:37-40.

302. Watson, G.W. 1986. *Cultural practices can influence root development for better transplanting success.* J. Environ. Hort. 4:32-34.

303. Watson, G.W. 1987. *Are auxins practical for B&B trees?* Am. Nurseryman. 166:183-184.

304. Watson, G.W. 1989. Getting more roots into the root ball, pp. 20-26, **In** Metria:6 Proceedings. Mentor, OH.

305. Watson, G.W. 1994. *Root growth response to fertilizers.* J. Arboric. 20:4-8.

306. Watson, G.W., S. Clark, and K. Johnson. 1990. *Formation of girdling roots.* J. Arboric. 16: 197-202.

307. Watson, G.W. and E.B. Himelick. 1982. *Seasonal variation in root regeneration of transplanted trees.* J. Arboric. 8:305-310.

308. Watson, G.W. and T.D. Sydnor. 1987. *The effect of root pruning on the root system of nursery trees.* J. Arboric. 13:126-130.

309. Wilde, S.A. 1958. Forest Soils Ronald Press, NY.

310. Wong, T.L., R.W. Harris, and R.E. Fissell. 1971. *Influence of high soil temperatures on five woody-plant species.* J. Am. Soc. Hort. Sci. 96:80-82.

311. Wright, R.A., R.W. Wein, and B.P. Dancik. 1992. *Population differentiation in seedling root size between adjacent stands of jack pine.* For. Sci. 38:777-785.

312. Yeager, T.H. and R.D. Wright. 1981. *Influence of nitrogen and phosphorous on shoot:root ratio of* Ilex crenata Thumb. Helleri. HortSci. 16:564-565.

313. Ziza, R.P., H.G. Halverson, and B.B. Stout. 1980. Establishment and early growth of conifers on compact soils in urban areas. USDA For. Ser. Res. Pap. NE-451.

chapter

9

Establishment in the Landscape

A newly planted tree or shrub will be under stress until its root system can fully develop at the new site. Water stress can occur even with the best of care, especially on hot, sunny days. The duration and severity of this post-planting stress is affected by many factors.

DEFINING POST-PLANTING STRESS

The term *transplanting shock* has often been used to describe the stress induced by transplanting. The dictionary defines a shock as a disturbance in equilibrium. While use of the term transplanting shock is technically correct for field-grown plants, *post-planting stress* more completely and directly describes the physiological condition of any recently planted tree or shrub.

Plant growth is always limited by the factor required for growth that is in shortest supply, even if all other factors are plentiful. Common limiting environmental factors are temperature, light, water, and nutrients. If no environmental factors are limiting, then plant growth will be limited only by the genetic potential of the plant (maximum possible growth rate).

After planting, water is usually the most limiting factor. Even if soil moisture is adequate, the root system may not be able to absorb water fast enough to completely satisfy the needs of the plant. Temperature, light, nutrients, and other factors are usually less limiting than water for the initial period after planting.

Recently planted trees and shrubs rely heavily on root ball soil moisture throughout the first growing season. For balled and burlapped plants, the moisture contained within the soil ball represents only a small fraction of the water that was available to the full root system before transplanting. Light container media will hold less water in the landscape (see Chapter 5), and once planted it will probably be irrigated less frequently than in the nursery. Both types of soil balls hold very little water relative to the transpiration demands of the plant. Figure 9-1 shows that root ball soil moisture can be depleted very quickly during the first season, while backfill soils just outside the root ball stay very moist. In temperate climates, it can take 4-5 months for enough roots to grow into the soil outside the root ball to absorb significant amounts of soil moisture (321,328). The water in the backfill soils is not able to move into the root ball quickly enough to replace what is being removed from the root ball soil by the roots. The root ball soil can reach -500 mbars of soil moisture tension in just a few days between waterings. This level of soil moisture is dry enough to stop root growth and reduce the capacity of the roots to absorb water because of increased suberization of root tips (317). It may take several days for roots to start growing again after watering. With frequent soil drying, periods when root growth is stopped may overlap. If root growth is stopped for long periods, the establishment period may be lengthened.

Calculating the amount of water held in the root zone in relation to usage by the plant is another way to look at the potential for water stress in new plantings. Table 9-1 shows that the moisture available to the expanding root systems of recently planted shrubs increases more rapidly than does water used by the

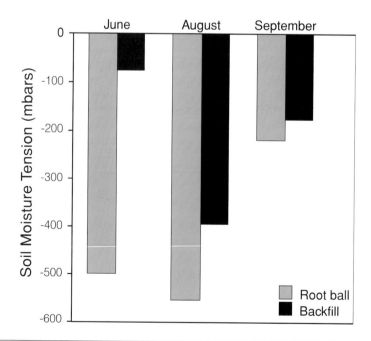

FIGURE 9-1. Transplanted trees rely almost entirely on root ball moisture for much of the first growing season. Root ball soils dry more rapidly (more negative indicates drier soil) while backfill soils remain moist. Not until near the end of the summer, 14 weeks after planting, did roots absorb significant amounts of water from the backfill soil, but still the root ball soil dried faster (after 328).

TABLE 9-1. Soil moisture available to the rapidly expanding roots system of newly planted 1 gal (4 L) container shrubs increases faster than transpirational water loss by the crown (315).

Weeks after planting	Water used per day (liters)	Water available in root zone (liters)	Water supply (days)
4	0.5	2	4
11	1.0	6	6
16	1.5	12	8
21	2.0	23	11

crown. Four weeks after planting, the shrubs required watering every 4 days. By 21 weeks after planting (the end of the first growing season), watering was required only once every 11 days. Because the root system had expanded into a much greater volume of soil, more water was available to it and the watering cycle could be extended (315). A woody plant may be considered established when the watering cycle can be extended to at least two weeks during warm, summer weather without substantial water stress. This occurred near the end of the second season for 2 in (5 cm) green ash (*Fraxinus pennsylvanica*) trees in hardiness zone 5 (328), and in about 6 months after planting laurel oak (*Quercus laurifolia*) in zone 9 (316).

Another way to determine when a plant is fully established is to compare growth rate before and after transplanting. Growth rate will slow immediately after transplanting and recover to pre-transplanting levels as the root system regenerates and post-planting stress is reduced (319,326) (Figure 9-2).

For species with only one flush of growth each year, twig growth may be smaller the second year after transplanting than the first year. Growth is influenced by conditions at the time the bud is forming and also at the time when the bud is expanding. The bud for the first year's growth after transplanting is large and contains many leaf primordia (preformed leaves) because it was formed under excellent conditions in the nursery. Because the bud expands under conditions of great stress, the expanded leaves are small and closely spaced. The bud for the second year's growth is formed under highly stressed conditions and may be much smaller with fewer leaves. Stress during the second year is somewhat reduced after one year of root growth, and the smaller bud is well matched with the moderate stress. Consequently, the leaves are nearer to normal size. Because the smaller bud results in fewer leaves, the annual growth extension may be actually smaller than the first year after transplanting (Figure 9-3). Each successive year, the conditions for bud formation and expansion are less stressful as the root system regenerates. The twig growth gets longer and longer until the tree is once again growing at the same rate as before transplanting, if the conditions are as favorable as they were in the nursery. For species with multiple flushes, or continual growth throughout the season, the changes will probably be more gradual.

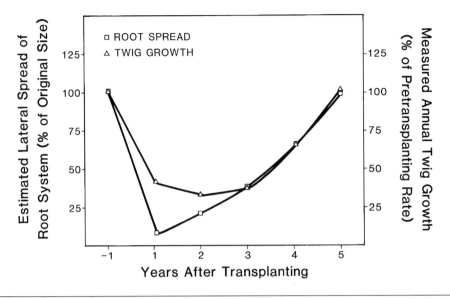

FIGURE 9-2. Root loss as a result of transplanting causes a corresponding decrease in twig growth. Recovery of twig growth rate is closely related to regeneration of the root system (326).

FIGURE 9-3. It is easy to see the pattern of growth after transplanting on evergreens because they retain several years of needles. Growth the first year (between arrows) is dwarfed, but with nearly as many needles as before transplanting. The second year there are fewer needles, but they are closer to normal size.

DURATION OF POST-PLANTING STRESS

To be considered *fully established*, the partial root system in the root ball, or the confined root system of the container, must develop into a normal spreading root system that can utilize soil moisture and nutrient resources from a large soil volume. This usually takes several years of root growth.

Tree size

Root system establishment takes longer for large trees than for small trees. When standard specifications are followed, the size of the root ball or container is proportional to the size of the plant. A similar small percentage of the root system is transplanted with the B&B or container root ball, regardless of plant size. Root extension rates are also similar for large and small trees. What is very different for the two sizes of trees is the distance that roots must grow to develop the full spreading root system necessary to fully establish on the new site. A smaller tree requires fewer annual root growth increments to replace the original root system after planting than does a large tree (Figure 9-4) (325).

What is the best size tree to plant? It can be different for every situation. Large trees can be transplanted very successfully, if a large tree is needed or wanted immediately. The larger the tree, the longer it will take to establish. A commitment to special maintenance (primarily watering) will be required throughout the longer establishment period or it may not survive. Both the cost of planting the tree and the cost of the maintenance will be higher. Sometimes a smaller tree is more appropriate. A small tree will be less expensive to purchase and plant and will establish more quickly. Extra watering may only be necessary for the first year or two. Because vigorous growth returns to a small tree sooner after transplanting, small and large trees planted at the same time may be similar in size by the time both are established (Figure 9-5) (318,322,323,324,325).

Species

Some species are known for their ease of transplanting, while others are known to be more difficult. Easy-to-transplant usually means excellent survival and fast to establish with minimal care, and it is usually related to rate of root regeneration (314). Table 2-3 lists the relative ease of transplanting for many species. Those that are more difficult-to-transplant, such as many oak species, may just be slower to establish and require more attention.

Climate

Root growth after transplanting is highly affected by soil temperature (see Chapter 8). In climates where the soils are warm all year round, roots will grow more rapidly and plants will become established sooner. In the north temperate climate of the upper Midwestern United States, twig growth of a 4 in (10 cm) caliper tree, is slowed for four years after transplanting (327). In other words, the establishment period is approximately one year per caliper inch. In the subtropical climate of northern Florida, roots grow much faster. Trees establish in

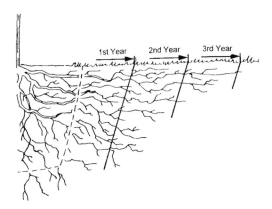

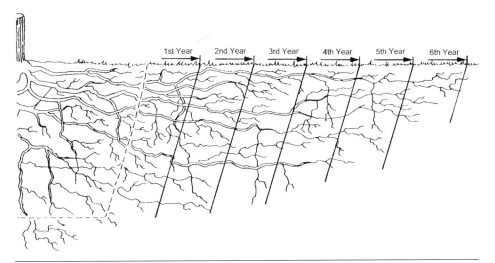

FIGURE 9-4.   Roots grow at a similar rate regardless of tree size, but for a larger tree, roots must grow over a longer distance to redevelop a normal root spread after transplanting. This requires more years of growth and results in a longer establishment period for a large tree.

approximately 3 months per caliper in (316,319). No data is available from other climates, but times can be approximated by comparing the length of the growing season, soil temperature, and soil type information.

Stress decreases and growth increases each year as the roots grow. During the second half of the establishment period, the tree may not appear to be stressed. Though stress is less severe and the associated growth reduction may not be as obvious, stress can still be measured. At this time, monitoring should be continued, but supplemental watering may be necessary only during dry periods.

Production method

Establishment of traditional field-grown trees with conventional root balls has been compared to container grown trees and trees grown in in-ground fabric containers. Based on water stress data, field-grown trees usually establish most

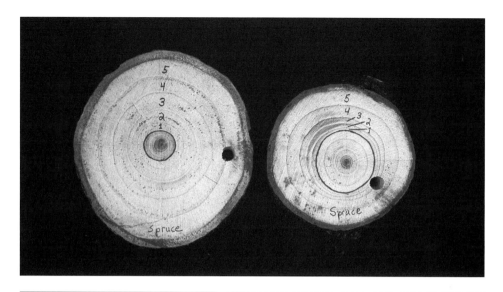

FIGURE 9-5. Trunk sections of transplanted spruces show that growth of the larger transplanted tree was slowed for several years (right, size at the time of transplanting is shown by the circle). Normal growth of the smaller tree (left) resumes more quickly. By the time vigorous growth returns to the larger tree, the smaller tree was larger in diameter.

quickly. Trees planted from plastic containers establish most slowly. Establishment of in-ground fabric bag trees is variable (316,320). Container plants were smaller and with minimal root loss at planting, yet took longer to become established. Smaller plants with a more balanced root-crown ratio might be expected to establish more quickly, but this was not the case.

Both periodic and chronic stress can reduce growth. If a plant receives a high level of care and a consistent environment is maintained above- and belowground, good growth will occur and the plant will establish faster. Proper care after planting will help to assure survival and to minimize stress.

LITERATURE CITED

314. Arnold, M.A. and D.K. Struve. 1989. *Cupric carbonate controls green ash root morphology and root growth.* HortSci. 24:262-264.
315. Barnett, D. 1986. *Root growth and water use by newly transplanted woody landscape plants.* Public Garden 1:23-25.
316. Beeson, R.C. and E.F. Gilman. 1992. *Diurnal water stress during landscape establishment of slash pine differs among three production methods.* J. Arboric. 18:281-286.
317. Bevington, K.B. and W.S. Castle. 1985. *Annual root growth pattern of young citrus trees in relation to shoot growth, soil temperature and soil water content.* J. Am. Soc. Hort. Sci 110:840-845.
318. Clemans, J. and S.P. Radford. 1986. *Establishment trials of ornamental trees and shrubs in coastal New South Wales.* J. Arboric. 10:117-123.

319. Gilman, E.F. and R.C. Beeson. 1996. *Production method affects tree establishment in the landscape.* J. Environ. Hort. 14:81-87.

320. Harris, J.R. and E.F. Gilman. 1993. *Production method affects growth and post-transplant establishment of* East Palatka *holly.* J.Am. Soc. Hort. Sci. 118:194-200.

321. Harris, J.R., P. Knight, and J. Fanelli. 1996. *Fall transplantibility of balled and burlapped fringe tree* (Chionanthus virginicus L.). HortSci. 31:1143-1145.

322. Lauderdale, D.M., C.H. Gilliam, D.J. Eakes, G.J. Keever, and A.H. Chappelka. 1995. *Tree transplant size influences post-transplant growth, gas exchange, and leaf water potential of* October Glory *red maple.* J. Environ. Hort. 13:178-181.

323. Litzow, M. and H. Pellet. 1982. *Establishment rates for different bareroot grades of trees.* J. Arboric. 8:264-266.

324. Vanstone, D.E. and W.G. Ronald. 1981. *Comparison of bare-root versus tree spade transplanting of boulevard trees.* J. Arboric. 7:271-274.

325. Watson, G. 1985. *Tree size affects root regeneration and top growth after transplanting.* J. Arboric. 11:37-40.

326. Watson, G.W. 1987. *The relationship of root growth and tree vigour following transplanting.* Arboricultural J. 11:97-104.

327. Watson, G.W., E.B. Himelick, and E.T. Smiley. 1986. *Twig growth of eight species of shade trees following transplanting.* J. Arboric. 12:241-245.

328. Watson, G.W. and G. Kupkowski. 1991. *Soil moisture uptake by green ash trees after transplanting.* J. Environ. Hort. 9:226-227.

Care After Planting

One of the most common causes of transplanting failure is inadequate care. During the time when the plant is adapting to its new site and growing new roots, it must be given a higher level of attention and maintenance. Water management on urban sites with poor soils is difficult, especially for new plants. Too much or too little water are probably responsible for the death of more plants in the urban landscape than any other factors.

Providing conscientious maintenance on a regular basis can help young plants to quickly mature into beautiful specimens. Often, the best horticultural care recreates critical aspects of the natural environment. Mulching is a good example. Some maintenance procedures, such as careful pruning, can represent an improvement over the natural system. Other measures are simply required because of urbanization. Lawn mower protection would never be required in the woodland.

Many common problems associated with transplanting can be minimized with vigilant maintenance. The type of care a plant needs changes as it overcomes post-planting stress to become a vigorous young plant, and then eventually a mature plant, but the need for maintenance will continue throughout the life of the plant.

chapter

10

Care After Planting

Maintenance after planting is an extension of the planting process itself, though people other than those who did the planting are usually responsible. Procedures such as watering, mulching, fertilizing, and pruning that were important at planting are also important afterwards. Starting immediately after planting, the tree will require special care for at least the first two years, longer for trees over 3 in (8 cm) caliper. From then on, it will require the same level of maintenance as other young established plants in the landscape.

REGULAR INSPECTIONS

Careful and regular observation of the plant's performance is very important. A newly planted tree or shrub is likely to develop leaves later in the spring than established plants, and the leaves may be smaller. The leaves may be slightly off color due to stress, but should not be showing signs of severe water stress (dull appearance or drooping). Twig growth may also be reduced, but the twigs should have no indication of shriveled bark. Watch the trunk for discolored sunken bark areas, sunscald, borers, cankers, and mechanical or animal damage. Check the soil in the root ball regularly to determine the amount of moisture. In the spring there may be too much soil water and in the summer there may not be enough. The transition between too wet and too dry may occur in as little as a week in many urban soils.

WATERING

Proper watering is the most important maintenance practice, but specific recommendations vary with different environmental conditions. Watering practices must vary with weather conditions. The amount and frequency of irrigation needed depends on the amount of rainfall, daily temperatures and wind conditions, moisture-holding capacity of the soil, drainage, and stage of root system establishment. If the soil is poorly drained, it is important not to apply too much water.

Root growth is slowed by dry soils (329,346). When roots are drought stressed, they mature rapidly toward the tip (suberization), decreasing absorption, and reducing future growth (335). Water stress during periods of root growth reduces the root-shoot ratio (336).

Transpiration rate may be very high in the first few days after transplanting (332,333,340). Adequate irrigation during this period is extremely important for survival. Overhead misting may help reduce stress for a few weeks after transplanting, but it is ineffective after the plant adjusts (330,331) and probably not worth the expense. Mild stress lasting ten days or less slows growth temporarily, but may not affect total season growth. Stress of 22 days or longer can reduce growth for both the current season and the following season (345).

In the first two years, the most important place to check the soil moisture is in the root ball. This is the major source of water for the tree until the root system regenerates. In hot summer weather, the root ball can become very dry in just two or three days, while the surrounding soil remains moist. Low-cost soil moisture meters are not very dependable or accurate. The best way to check root ball soil moisture is to sample the soil with a soil profile tube (Figure 10-1). A soil profile tube removes a small core of soil that can be easily examined, but the number of times one can be inserted into a small root ball may be limited. If the soil retains its shape after compressing it between the fingers, but is not sticky, the moisture content is favorable. Soil taken from closer to the surface of the root ball with a hand trowel can be tested in the same way, but the soil deeper in the root ball may be wetter or drier. Determining soil resistance by probing the soil ball and the backfill with a pointed metal rod (such as a common root-watering needle without the water running) can also be used to estimate soil moisture. Very dry soil will resist penetration of the rod and indicate the need for watering. If suction develops that resists removal of the rod, and the rod surface is wet when removed, then the soil is too wet. The first few times it is very helpful to compare rod resistance to soil samples removed with a core, or by digging with a hand trowel. After a little practice, the rod method of determining soil moisture can be easy and accurate.

On sites where excess moisture can be a severe problem, a small 1-2 in (2.5-5.0 cm) plastic pipe can be inserted outside of the soil ball to the bottom of the planting hole where the water level can be checked with a wooden dowel used as a dip stick (Figure 10-2). On very wet sites, drainage may have to be provided (see Chapter 3).

To water the root ball, apply water slowly near the base of the plant, or use a root-watering needle under low pressure. The hose or needle may have to be moved to several locations for large root balls. Commercially manufactured bags designed to hold water and release it slowly can be helpful when placed over the root ball if soil absorbs water very slowly. They can also be used to apply a measured amount of water. Water applied too rapidly is lost through run-off.

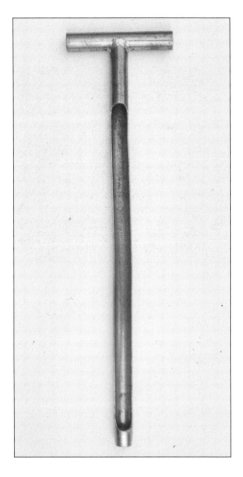

FIGURE 10-1. A soil profile tube is a handy tool for removing cores from the upper 10-14 in (35-36 cm) of soil.

FIGURE 10-2. On wet sites, vertical pipes can be installed in the planting hole to check for excess water with a dipstick. The water can be pumped out if it is practical and necessary for plant survival.

A raised ring of soil at the edge of the root ball (not the edge of the planting hole) will help to keep water from running off of the root ball.

Throughout the warm, summer weather, the tree will probably need water about twice each week. Summer showers usually do little to moisten the root ball. Ten gal (40 l) of water or less, will probably be sufficient to thoroughly wet a 20-24 in (50-60 cm) diameter root ball. The exact amount will vary with the soil type and extent of dryness. Do not over water. Applying more water will not keep the root ball moist any longer. The excess water will move into the surrounding soil that is already moist, and the water will not be able to move back into the root ball as fast as moisture is absorbed by the plant. Daily watering with just 1 gal (4 l) of water per inch of trunk caliper might provide the most even soil moisture for roots. The time required to deliver the appropriate amount of water from a hose can easily be measured by filling a similar sized container. Use the same pressure when watering. Watering should be continued through the fall season, though the frequency may be reduced. Plants should go into the winter with ample moisture in the soil, especially evergreens.

As the root system establishes, the frequency of watering can be reduced and the area watered can be enlarged. There may be fewer roots and greater stress on the south side of the tree (343,344). Increased irrigation may be appropriate on the south side to compensate. The average increase in root spread radius can be from 1.5-6 ft (0.5-2 m) per year depending on climate (north temperate to subtropical, respectively) and site conditions (Table 10-1). Using these generalized growth rates, irrigation frequency can be reduced when the root spread is three times the root ball diameter, but the irrigation should not be completely stopped. One gallon of water per square foot of soil surface area within and just beyond

TABLE 10-1. The estimated root spread diameter of a transplanted tree can be used to determine the appropriate area to water, fertilize, and mulch each year as the root system grows. Root spread estimation is based on a 24 in (60 cm) diameter root ball and favorable growing conditions. Make adjustments as necessary for root ball size and growing conditions.

| Climate | Years after transplanting | | | |
	1	2	3	4
Subtropical (Hardiness zones 9-11)	14(4.3)*	26(8)	38(11.7)	**
Mild winters, long summers (Hardiness zones 6-8)	8(2.5)	14(4.3)	20(6.15)	26(8)
Cold winters, short summers (Hardiness zones 4-5)	5(1.5)	8(2.8)	11(3.4)	14(4.3)

* feet (meters)
** all but the largest trees will be established

the root zone should be a general guide to provide a sufficient volume of water when irrigation is required.

When numerous trees and shrubs are planted in a large bed, an alternative to watering each individual root ball may be necessary. Overhead irrigation with sprinklers may be possible with ample drainage. At an appropriate interval (determined by checking root ball and bed soil moisture), apply the equivalent of 2 in (5 cm) of rainfall slowly enough that it is all absorbed by the soil. Measure the amount of water applied with a wide container with straight sides. Another alternative is a drip irrigation system. The components are available at most landscape supply houses and home centers. Emitters can be placed at each root ball. Larger root balls will require multiple emitters or types with higher flow rate and a wider area of application.

Irrigation systems not properly calibrated and monitored cause the death of many landscape plants. When trees and shrubs are irrigated the same amount and frequency as nearby lawn areas, too much irrigation water can be applied. Shady locations may receive the same irrigation as sunny locations. Irrigation cycles are often not adjusted for heavy rainfall that may occur.

FERTILIZATION

As long as no nutrient deficiency exists in the soil, fertilization may be unnecessary for at least the first growing season after planting. Moderate release of nutrients by decomposition of both mulch and organic matter added to backfill soil may be sufficient during this initial establishment period.

As the plant develops a greater absorptive root area and becomes more established, higher fertility levels may be desired to maximize growth. A reliable soil test performed as part of the initial site evaluation will be useful in indicating any deficiencies in essential nutrients. Because nitrogen exists in so many forms, and is so short-lived in the soil, standard soil tests do not include it. Plant growth is more often limited by a deficiency of nitrogen than by any other element, and it may need to be added annually to maintain an optimum supply for maximum growth.

Starting the beginning of the second season after planting (third season for large trees), fertilizer can be applied to the root zone (see Table 10-1). The root zone will increase in size faster in a warmer climate. Research has shown that up to 6 lb. of actual nitrogen per 1000 sq ft is effective in improving growth of trees once they are established (334,338,341,342). Formulations and application methods vary according to the type of fertilizer to be applied. Phosphorous, potassium, and other non-mobile elements are most effective when applied below the soil surface. Slow release fertilizer formulations can be applied during the fall and winter, and the nutrients will still be available the following spring when they are most effective (337). Professional arborists often use liquid injection of slow release formulations. Small amounts of the fertilizer should be injected in many locations in the upper 4-6 in (10-15 cm) of the soil where most of the fine roots are located. Homeowners can apply nitrogen effectively by broadcasting granular fertilizer on the soil surface in the spring, and it will readily move down to the roots. Granular fertilizer applied in drilled holes may not be as effective since the nutrients are concentrated in limited areas. Lawn fertilizers containing broadleaf weed killers and other herbicides should not be used in the vicinity of any tree or shrub. Some weed killers can be absorbed by the roots and become systemic. They are then translocated to rapidly growing portions of the tree or shrub where they can cause injury or death.

MULCHING

Mulch applied at planting time will need to be replenished and expanded from time to time. As the organic mulch decomposes, new mulch must be added periodically. Every couple of years, as the new root system spread further, the mulched area should be expanded in diameter (Table 10-1), and about 2 in (5 cm) of new mulch will also need to be added to the previously established area.

As the mulched area expands, compatible plantings may be added to enhance the landscape appearance. Most trees can tolerate root competition from woody shrubs, groundcovers, and even some perennials. Woodland plant communities are a mix of these kinds of plants, and they should pose no threat in the landscape. When planting in the root zone of existing trees, disturb as little soil as possible to minimize damage to the roots of the tree. Each autumn shredded leaves can be added to the mulch, recycling the nutrients and organic matter, just as in the forest.

TRUNK PROTECTION

Basal trunk damage from lawn mowers and weed whips is a serious problem in landscapes. The bark on young trees is thin and very susceptible to mechanical damage. Because of post-planting stress, the cambium around a small wound can dieback further and become a more serious injury. Home-made and commercially available trunk guards are highly recommended to prevent mechanical injury to the trunk and to prevent small rodent damage (see Chapter 7). A well-maintained mulched area should completely eliminate the need to use mechanical tools around all trees.

Large animals such as beaver and deer can cause major trunk and branch damage. Heavy hardware cloth, chicken wire, or metal fencing covering the bottom three feet of the trunk will provide protection against beaver, unless snow is deep. Protect the trunk with plastic drainpipe in the fall to prevent antler rubbing by deer. Golf courses use 5-6 ft sections of corrugated plastic drainpipe to protect tree trunks from golf balls. White plastic is best if the guards are used in the summer months.

Trunk wraps can cause damage. Moisture held under the wraps has been linked to increases in bark splitting. The injured bark can serve as an entrance point for canker fungi, and the wrap may increase incidence of borers (339). Trunk wraps and guards can cause physical injury to the trunk if left on too long (Figures 10-3 and 10-4). In northern climates, it is best to apply trunk wraps for

FIGURE 10-3.   In one season, burlap caused constriction of the trunk, and an imprint of the fiber pattern in the bark of this tree.

winter sun protection, but remove them during the growing season. In hot and dry climates, protection from summer sun may be more important, but it may be necessary to loosen the wrap at least once during the growing season to prevent trunk constriction, borer activity, excess moisture, or canker formation. The same paper may be used to rewrap the tree if the paper is still in good condition.

Any supporting wires around the trunk should be checked frequently and adjusted to prevent trunk girdling and excessive wind movement until they can be permanently removed. **Stakes on smaller trees can often be removed after one year.** A good test is to move the trunk back and forth to determine if the tree trunk is rigid at the soil line and the root ball soil does not move. Re-examine the supports annually until the stakes can be removed. If stakes are required to hold the tree upright for more than one year, the roots are not growing properly. Check for site problems or maintenance practices that could be limiting root system development.

FIGURE 10-4. A spiral plastic tree guard caused damage to this trunk when not removed as the tree grew. (photo credit - D. Rideout)

PRUNING

Pruning small trees for proper branch structure should continue in the years after planting. Periodic removal of older stems of shrubs is an ongoing process. Shrubs that were cut back completely will need to have the new sprouts thinned.

Final permanent branch spacing (up to 18 in (45 cm) depending on mature size of the tree) may not be possible until the tree has grown larger. Inspect soundness of branch attachments regularly. Prune out any branches with weak crotches, dieback that may develop, and sprouts along the trunk and from the rootstock below the graft union.

PEST CONTROL

Insect and disease control measures may periodically be required. Plants in a stressed condition following planting are susceptible to many diseases and insects, especially borers. When necessary, a fungicide or insecticide may be applied. Only registered chemicals should be used and spraying must be done according to the instructions on the label.

Planting a tree or shrub is a simple concept, but it is by no means a simple process. In nature, many seeds fall and only a few of the stronger seeds that land in a favorable location develop into a mature tree. In the landscape, survival rates must be better — as close to 100 percent as possible. **To achieve this high level of success, the "right tree" must be in the "right place" and receive the "right care" — the three basic elements of planting trees and shrubs successfully.**

LITERATURE CITED

329. Barnett, D. 1986. *Root growth and water use by newly transplanted woody landscape plants.* The Public Garden. April: 23-25.

330. Bates, R.M. and A.X. Niemiera. 1994. *Mist irrigation reduces post-transplant desiccation of bare-root trees.* J. Environ. Hort. 12:1-3.

331. Beeson R.C. and E.F. Gilman. 1992. *Water stress and osmotic adjustment during post-digging acclimation of* Quercus virginiana *produced in fabric containers.* J. Environ. Hort. 10:208-214.

332. Clemens, J. and S.P. Radford. 1986. *Establishment trials of ornamental trees and shrubs in coastal New South Wales.* J. Arboric. 10:117-123.

333. Harris, J.R. and E.F. Gilman. 1995. *Production method affects growth and post-transplant establishment of* East Palatka *holly.* J.Am. Soc. Hort. Sci. 118:194-200.

334. Himelick, E.B., D. Neely, and W.R. Crowley, Jr. 1965. *Experimental field studies on shade tree fertilization.* Illinois Nat. Hist. Survey Biological Notes. 53. 12 pp.

335. Kaufman, M.R. 1968. *Water relations of pine seedlings in relation to root and shoot growth.* Plant Physiol. 43:281-288.

336. McMillin, J.D. and M.R. Wagner. 1995. *Effects of water stress on biomass partitioning of* Ponderosa *pine seedlings during primary root growth and shoot growth periods.* For. Sci. 41:594-610.

337. Neely, D. and E.B. Himelick. 1987. *Fertilizing and watering trees.* Illinois Nat. Hist. Survey Circular 56. Third revision. 24 pp.

338. Neely, D., E.B. Himelick, and W.R. Crowley, Jr. 1970. Fertilization of Established Trees: A Report of Field Studies. Illinois Nat. Hist. Survey Bulletin Vol. 30, Article 4.

339. Owen, N.P., C.S. Sador, and J.J. Raupp. 1991. *The effect of plastic tree wrap on borer incidence in dogwood.* J. Arboric. 17:29-31.

340. Rook, D.A. 1973. *Conditioning* radiata pine *seedlings to transplanting by restricted watering.* N.Z.J. For. Sci. 3:54-69.

341. Watson, G.W. and E.B. Himelick. 1982. *Root distribution of nursery trees and its relationship to transplanting success.* J. Arboric. 8:225-229.

342. Williams, J.D., H.G. Ponder, and C.H. Gilliam. 1987. *Response of* Cornus florida *to moisture stress.* J. Arboric. 13:98-101.

343. Witherspoon, W.R. and G.P. Lumis. 1986. *Root Regeneration of* Tilia cordata *cultivars after transplanting in response to root exposure and soil moisture levels.* J. Arboric. 12:165-168.
344. van de Werken, H. 1980. *Fertilization and other factors enhancing the growth rate of young shade trees.* J. Arboric. 7:33-37.
345. van de Werken, H. 1984. *Fertilization practices as they influence the growth rate of young shade trees.* J. Environ. Hort. 2:64-69.
346. von der Heide-Spravka, K.G., and G.W. Watson. 1990. *Directional variation in growth of trees.* J. Arboric. 16:169-173.

Common Problems of Recently Planted Trees

Many problems of newly planted trees and shrubs are related to post-planting stress. Post-planting stress can predispose plants to certain stress related problems that otherwise would not be of major concern. The care provided by the new owner could have a substantial effect in reducing and preventing these stress related problems. Uninformed homeowners and careless maintenance workers can be the cause of a few problems that are unrelated to stress. Becoming familiar with these common problems can aid in recognizing them early and minimizing the potential damage.

STRESS RELATED PROBLEMS

Certain pest and physiological problems occur more frequently on stressed plants. The specific reasons for this are not always understood. Minimizing stress by judicious watering can minimize or eliminate many problems.

Borers

The larval stage of various flying adult insects is called borers. The adult female often lays its eggs in bark crevices, and occasionally in scar tissue around wounds of the host plant. After the eggs hatch, the young larvae burrow through the bark leaving very little evidence of entry. Some bore deeply into the wood; others make serpentine galleries in the cambium area, between the bark and outer wood. These damaged areas interfere with the transport of water, minerals and nutrients up and down the trunk. Galleries can encircle the entire trunk or branch, killing everything beyond it. Pupation occurs the following season and adults

emerge to start the cycle over. The entry and exit holes are sometimes filled with sawdust and may have a gummy ooze flowing from the hole. There is usually one generation per year.

Prevention is the key in controlling wood-boring insect pests. Mulch and regular watering will reduce stress. Chemical sprays can be used on the trunk and major branches as protectants from borer attack.

Cankers

Localized dead areas on the trunk and branches caused by fungi are called cankers. Cankers occur when the vascular cambium on a portion of the stem is killed. Usually this leaves a depressed and discolored area with a definite margin. On conifers, resin may ooze from the canker and accumulate on the surface.

The canker slows or prevents transport of water and minerals upward in the wood and nutrients downward in the bark. They may structurally weaken the plant and can provide an entry point for wood-decay fungi. Cankers are destructive when they develop around large areas of the trunk or branches.

The most frequent damage to trees results from fungi that

persist as saprophytes on the bark of vigorous trees, but become pathogenic on stressed trees with low vigor. Canker fungi can enter through wounds, including those caused by insect borers. Cankers can enlarge rapidly as long as the host tree has low vigor and remains under stress. The best way to prevent cankers is to minimize stress and avoid wounds and bruises on the bark.

Sunscald

A strip of dead bark on the trunk resulting from excessive warming by direct sun is known as sunscald. Damage is usually on the south or southwest sides. In cold climates the cause is most often attributed to a period of warm winter air temperatures and the sun warming the bark followed by a sudden drop in temperature and rapid freezing of the cambium. In warmer climates, exposure to intense summer sun is thought to cause damage. Excessive and continued water stress can make bark susceptible to serious dehydration from high temperatures. Trunk wraps are commonly used to shield the bark and prevent sunscald, though research data supporting their effectiveness is lacking. Trunks should be wrapped from the bottom to the top so that the overlapping layers shed water. Wrapping materials are best left in place only during the season when damage is likely to occur. If left in place during the growing season, they should be removed periodically to inspect the trunk and loosen the wrap so that the growing trunk is not constricted (see Chapter 10).

Leaf tatter

Irregular holes appearing on the leaves of broadleaf plants in spring are known as leaf tatter. The epidermal leaf cells are injured while the leaves are rapidly expanding. The young leaves of plants are very tender and the symptoms are often first observed on warm, sometimes windy early spring days. Small irregular dead areas develop around major leaf veins. The areas become larger as the leaf expands. Leaf tatter can occur on many plant species and is commonly observed on newly planted trees and shrubs. The damage is often mistaken for insects feeding on the leaves. Though not usually a serious problem, in extreme cases leaf damage can be severe and significantly reduce leaf area and photosynthesis. There presently is no known prevention for leaf tatter. Other minor leaf problems (leaf spot disease, insect feeding, etc.) are inevitable on all trees and shrubs. These are also not a serious problem unless a substantial amount of leaf area is lost.

Excessive needle drop

Heavier than normal loss of needles is common on recently planted evergreens. Evergreens typically loose their oldest interior needles each year, usually in the fall. The number of needles remaining on the tree varies with species. Some pines keep only two years of needles, while some spruces may keep many more. Stress can cause any plant to loose more needles than normal. An unusually large number of brown or yellow older needles are first noticed. After the needles fall, the plant may look unusually thin. If only the older needles are affected, this heavy loss of needles is usually not a major problem. After the plant has recovered from the stress, the normal number of needles will be retained. The needles may also be smaller the first year.

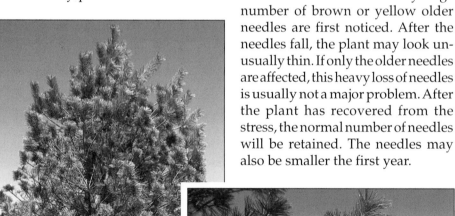

CULTURE RELATED PROBLEMS

Inadequate maintenance can be responsible for some problems. Carelessness can result in injury that can affect the tree for years.

Improper water management

Poor performance of recently planted trees and shrubs is often caused by too much or too little water. Poor drainage or excess watering (especially from irrigation systems) causes anaerobic (low oxygen) soils, killing the small absorbing roots. Without healthy roots to absorb water, the crown actually experiences a lack of water. Consequently, the symptoms can be similar to drought stress — dull or drooping leaves and branch tips, scorched leaf margins, and eventual dieback.

The entire root system may not be subjected to too much water. Roots in the lower portion of the root ball are often killed, and then stress is even more severe during subsequent dry periods. Aboveground, plant growth will be greatly reduced and show typical symptoms of water stress. Dieback may be so severe that the plant must be replaced.

Watering too infrequently during hot and dry summer weather can cause severe drought stress. Root ball soil moisture of B&B plants can be absorbed by the plant roots in just a few days. Container root balls may dry out in just a few hours on a hot summer day. With no roots yet developing into the surrounding soil, severe drought stress can occur rapidly. Soil moisture in the root ball should be monitored regularly and water applied as required (see Chapter 10). Mulching will reduce evaporation of soil moisture.

Mechanical damage

Mowers and string trimmers can easily damage the thin bark at the base of a small tree and damage is very common on newly planted trees. Stress can cause the wounds to enlarge and make the entry of canker and decay pathogens more likely. Mulch circles and plastic guards are very effective in preventing this kind of damage (see Chapter 7). (See examples on next page.)

Typical lawn mover damage. Cut section shows extent of injury and rot.

Animal damage

Various kinds of small and large rodents will gnaw the bark, girdling entire stems. The damage sometimes occurs below snow, tall grass, or mulch that provide protective cover from predators. Larger animals can chew off entire stems. Do not pile mulch or allow tall grass to grow around the base of the trunk. Trees and shrubs can be protected with cages of wire cloth. Tree trunks can also be protected with flexible drain tubing or commercially available products. The protection should be appropriate for the problem animals and take into consideration the height of the anticipated snow accumulation in winter. Repellent sprays may be effective but short-lived and must be reapplied periodically. Some plants are less susceptible to certain kinds of animal damage than others. Select plants that are known to have minimal problems.

Trunk girdling

Wires, guards, and cords left around the trunk of a tree or shrub can begin to constrict the bark in just one year, especially if the tree starts to grow rapidly. They often go unnoticed until it is too late. Synthetic cord is often carelessly left around the base of the trunk and it may be buried several inches deep in mulch and soil. The first observable symptom may be reduced twig and leaf vigor and enlarged trunk growth above the girdled area where a wire or cord was not removed. If discovered in time, removing the wire or cord will allow the plant to eventually recover.

ROOT RELATED PROBLEMS

Root problems originating in the nursery, or at planting time, may not be discovered until several years after planting. At least some excavation will be required to identify the problem. Sometimes, the cause cannot be identified until after the plant has died and is dug up.

Improper planting depth

One of the major causes of planting failure is planting too deep. Some contributing factors originate in the nursery, and others are the result of improper planting. Problems related to planting depth would occur most often on poorly drained sites. The visible symptoms are non-specific, just a general lack of vigor and eventual decline. Prevention through proper planting is imperative since it is very difficult to correct this problem without digging up the plant and replanting it at a higher level. Removing soil down to the root flare and creating a shallow, wide depression may help oxygen to reach the roots and improve vigor somewhat. Creating a small ring of raised soil around the depression will help keep surface water from flowing into the low area. Planting too shallow can also be a problem. This can easily occur when the root ball is raised excessively high trying to solve a poor drainage problem. The root ball may dry out quickly during dry periods, and roots may become exposed.

The tree illustrated was planted too deep, overwatered, and was dug with an extreemly small root system for a 1 in diameter tree. This tree had no chance for survival.

Circling roots

Plants produced in containers may have circling roots. Like most other root problems, aboveground symptoms are a general lack of vigor, chlorotic leaves, and slow decline. If discovered in time, it may be possible to disrupt the circling roots and replant the tree or shrub, but if vigor is already low, the plant should be replaced (see Chapter 5).

Poor root development

Seedlings with inferior root architecture develop into trees with low vigor and are not always culled in the nursery. These plants may never regain normal vigor after planting. If planted as a single tree, the low vigor may go unnoticed. As part of a group planting, a slow growing tree will become quite obvious as the others grow faster. Inferior root structure is often of genetic origin, and there is little that can be done after the tree is planted except to replace it. Improper planting can also result in poor root development. If the roots were not properly spread out at the bare root planting stage, kinked or clubbed roots may develop.

There may be other common problems on newly planted trees and shrubs in different regions. Check with the local cooperative extension or other local resources for more information.

appendix

B

Definitions

The nursery has developed standard terms for the procedures used to grow and harvest nursery stock.[1]

Growing systems

Nursery grown - Plants that are field-grown in a managed nursery under favorable growing conditions and that have received proper cultural treatment to develop a well branched root system.

Plantation grown - Plants that have been systematically planted in fertile, friable soil, but where plants have received minimal maintenance.

Collected - Plants growing in their native state with unrestricted root development and varying soil conditions. These plants are harvested with a larger minimum root spread if harvested as bare root plants, or with larger root balls if harvested as balled and burlapped plants. Collected trees grown in the nursery for two years or more are considered nursery grown.

Container grown - Plants grown in pots in the nursery since propagation, usually in light soil-less media or a combination of soil and media. They may be transplanted to larger pots several times before they are ready for market.

In-ground fabric bag grown - Plants that are field-grown in non-woven fabric bags, commonly called root control bags or grow bags.

Harvesting methods

Bare root - Nursery grown plants that are harvested and shipped without soil, usually of small caliper.

---

[1] After definitions in the American Standard for Nursery Stock. 1996. American Association of Nurserymen. Washington, D.C., 57 pp.

Processed balled - Plants dug bare root while dormant to which a growing media is added around the roots to form a ball designed to sustain plant growth until planted.

Balled and burlapped - Nursery grown plants that are hand dug or machine dug with a ball of earth and wrapped with burlap, twine, or other supporting systems.

Balled and potted (containerized) - Nursery grown plants dug with a ball of earth and placed in a container in lieu of burlapping.

appendix

C

Information for the Owner of a New Tree

Watering Trees and General Tree Care

Every tree should be watered at the time of planting to settle the soil and to assure adequate soil moisture. The planting crew may water it the first time. Afterwards, the property owner must provide water unless there has been sufficient rain to keep the soil moist. Watering must be continued throughout the growing season in temperate climates and year around in tropical and subtropical climates.

Trees must be watered regularly for 2 or 3 years after transplanting to provide adequate soil moisture while root systems are becoming established, longer for trees over 4 in (10 cm) caliper. A newly planted tree is most easily watered if a raised ring of soil 4 in (10 cm) high is formed around the edge of the root ball to create a "basin" or "saucer" for water. The saucer should be filled with 6 to 8 gal of water–4 gal per in (6 L per cm) for trees over 3 in (8 cm)–twice each week during periods of hot, dry weather; once each week during cooler, wetter periods. Brief, heavy showers may do little to help wet the root ball. Most of the water in the basin will soak into the root ball where the water is needed the most. To determine the need for watering, remove a small amount of soil at the edge of the ball with a hand trowel and squeeze it. If you can form a moist sticky ball, it is too wet. If it crumbles like chalk it is too dry. Disturbed soils are frequently high in clay and tend to drain poorly. If these conditions exist, allowing the water hose to run for prolonged periods of time in the reservoir will result in overwatering and cause the roots to drown from lack of soil aeration. **Adding large quantities of water too frequently to heavy clay soils is detrimental and may result in death of the tree.** Conversely, waiting to water until the tree wilts and the leaves start to turn brown is too late.

Future Advice

Leave the basin for watering the tree in place for 2 years before removing it. It may have to be repaired from time to time. Applying 2-4 in (5-10 cm) of wood chip or composted leaf mulch over the planting hole (inside and outside the soil ring) is beneficial because the mulch conserves soil moisture and encourages root development. Mulching also reduces weed development in the reservoir and eliminates mowing near the trunk. The lawn mower or weed whip should never come into contact with the tree trunk. Bark injury can result, causing poor growth and sometimes the death of the tree in later years.

Weed killers or lawn fertilizers that contain weed killers should not be used in the vicinity of trees, shrubs or flowerbeds. A top dressing of regular lawn fertilizer broadcast over the root area is beneficial when applied during March or April the second year of planting. One cup of fertilizer should cover an area 3 ft x 3 ft (1 m x 1 m).

appendix

D

Statements in this section are supported by complete discussions of the various subjects in the preceding chapters. Anyone using these specification guidelines would benefit from thorough study of the book.

Guide for Developing Planting Specifications

I. **General**

    A. Bidding requirements, general and special conditions, and other special requirements are hereby made part of the general specifications.

    B. Standard specifications of technical or professional societies and federal agencies referred to shall include all amendments as of the date of advertisement for bids.

II. **Time, Manner, and Requirements for Submitting Bids**

    A. Bidding requirements shall conform to the requirements of the contract forms and the specific requirements of these planting specifications.

    B. Bids filed for work under this section shall be for complete work. Bids shall be filed in a sealed envelope on the date specified in the advertisement until 12:00 noon, at which time the bids will be publicly opened and read.

III. **Description of Work**

These specifications include standards necessary for and incidental to the execution and completion of planting, including hauling and spreading of topsoil, and finished grading as indicated on the prepared drawings and specified herein.

    A. Specifications for excavation, filling, and rough grading: _____

    B. Protection of existing features. During construction, protect all existing trees, shrubs, and other **specified** vegetation, site features and improvements, structures, and utilities specified herein and/or on submitted drawings. Removal or destruction of existing plantings is prohibited unless specifically authorized by the owner.

IV.   Applicable Specifications and Standards

A. *Principles and Practice of Planting Trees and Shrubs.* 1997. International Society of Arboriculture, P.O. Box GG, Savoy, IL 61874.

B. *American Standard for Nursery Stock.* 1996. American Association of Nurserymen, Inc., 1250 I Street. N.C. Suite 500, Washington, D.C. 20005.

C. *Standardized Plant Names.* 1942. American Joint Committee on Horticulture Nomenclature, Horace McFarland Company, Harrisburg, Pennsylvania. (Second edition).

V.   Planting Season

(NOTE: Planting season varies with region, climatic conditions, type of nursery stock, and other factors. Insert the appropriate planting dates for your region.)

A. Planting shall be done within the following dates:

Deciduous trees and shrubs _____ to _____ .

Evergreen trees and other _____ to _____ .

Exceptions: _____ .

B. Variance: If special conditions exist that warrant a variance in the above planting dates, a written request shall be submitted to _____ stating the special conditions and the proposed variance. Permission for the variance will be given if warranted in the opinion of _____ .

VI.   Planting Locations

A. The landscape contractor (hereafter referred to as Contractor) shall plant at locations to be determined and marked by the owner, the arborist, urban forester, landscape architect, or other person representing the owner (hereafter referred to as the Owner's Representative).

B. Locations for individual trees will be supplied by the Owner's Representative. In some cases, the location may be inferred from reference to some identifiable field object or from some line that can be constructed in the field.

C. No tree that grows over 20 ft at maturity shall be planted under aerial utility wires.

D. No tree or shrub shall be planted within ___ ft of fire hydrants, driveways, street lights, or intersections, or as specified by local ordinance.

VII.   Utility Verification

(NOTE: This section is important because the Contractor may be responsible for damages to any unmarked utility. Downtime on some downtown computer phone lines can run thousands of dollars per minute.)

A. The Contractor shall contact the local utility companies for verification of the location of all underground utility lines in the area of the work. The Contractor shall be responsible for all damage resulting from neglect or failure to comply with this requirement.

B. Trees shall not be planted closer than ____ ft from water service con-
nections, sewer laterals, or gas lines, unless so directed by the Owner's
Representative. The Contractor shall be responsible for moving trees
if planted closer than the specified distance.

VIII. Materials

A. Topsoil will be furnished and hauled by _____ to the site.
The topsoil shall be declared by the Contractor to be free from subsoil,
roots, stones over 1 in (2.5 cm) in diameter, herbicides, contaminants,
and other extraneous materials. Materials removed shall be disposed
of by the Contractor. Topsoil shall be of granular structure, less than
27 percent clay, and 4 to 5 percent organic matter (by weight). Topsoil
shall not be used in a frozen or muddy condition. All surplus materials shall be removed by the Contractor.

B. Plants shall be true to species and variety specified, and nursery-
grown in accordance with good horticultural practices under climatic
conditions similar to those in the locality of the project for at least 2
years. They shall have been freshly dug (during the most recent favorable harvest season).

Unless specifically noted, all plants shall be of specimen quality,
exceptionally heavy, symmetrical, so trained or favored in development and appearance as to be unquestionably and outstandingly
superior in form, compactness, and symmetry. They shall be sound,
healthy, vigorous, well-branched and densely foliated when in leaf;
free of disease and insects, eggs, or larvae; and shall have healthy,
well-developed root systems. They shall be free from physical damage or other conditions that would prevent vigorous growth.

Trees with multiple leaders, unless specified, will be rejected.
Trees with a damaged or crooked leader, bark abrasions, sunscald,
disfiguring knots, insect damage, or cuts of limbs over 3/4 in (2 cm)
in diameter that are not completely closed will be rejected.

Plants shall conform to the measurements specified, except that
plants larger than those specified may be used if approved by the
Owner's Representative. Use of larger plants shall not increase the
contract price. If larger plants are approved, the root ball shall be
increased in proportion to the size of the plant.

Caliper measurements shall be taken on the trunk 6 in (15 cm)
above the natural ground line for trees up to and including 4 in (10
cm) in caliper, and 12 in (30 cm) above the natural ground line for trees
over 4 in (10 cm) in caliper. Height and spread dimensions specified
refer to the main body of the plant and not from branch tip to branch
tip. Plants shall be measured when branches are in their normal position. If a range of size is given, no plant shall be less than the minimum size, and no less than 50 percent of the plants shall be as large
as the maximum size specified. Measurements specified are minimum size acceptable after pruning, where pruning is required. Plants
that meet measurements but do not possess a standard relationship

between height and spread, according to the American Standards for Nursery Stock, shall be rejected.

Substitutions of plant materials will not be permitted unless authorized in writing by the Owner's Representative. If proof is submitted in writing that a plant specified is not obtainable, consideration will be given to the nearest available size or similar variety with a corresponding adjustment of the contract price.

C. The plant list at the end of this section is for the Contractor's information only, and no guarantee is expressed or implied that quantities therein are correct or that the list is complete. The Contractor shall satisfy himself that all plant materials shown on the drawings are included in his bid.

D. All plants shall be labeled by plant name and size. Labels shall be attached securely to all plants, bundles, and containers of plant materials when delivered. Plant labels shall be durable and legible, with information given in weather-resistant ink or embossed process lettering.

E. Certificates of Plant Inspections: Certificates of inspection shall accompany invoices for each shipment of plants as may be required by law for transportation. Certificates are to be filed with the Owner's Representative prior to acceptance of the material. Passing inspection by federal or state governments at place of growth does not preclude rejection of plants at the work site.

IX. Selection and Tagging

A. Plants shall be subject to inspection for conformity to specification requirements and approval by the Owner's Representative at their place of growth and upon delivery. Such approval shall not impair the right of inspection and rejection during progress of the work. Inspection outside the state of _____ shall be made at the expense of the Contractor. A Contractor's representative shall be present at all inspections.

B. A written request for the inspection of plant material at their place of growth shall be submitted to the Owner's Representative at least 10 calendar days prior to digging. This request shall state the place of growth and the quantity of plants to be inspected. The Owner's Representative may refuse inspection at this time if, in his/her judgment, sufficient quantities of plants are not available for inspection.

C. All plants shall be selected and tagged by the owner at their place of growth. For distant material, photographs may be submitted for pre-inspection review.

X. Digging and Handling Plant Materials

A. Antitranspirants, if specified, are to be applied to plants in full leaf immediately before digging. A film shall adequately cover all foliage.

B. Trees designated B&B shall be properly dug with firm natural balls of soil retaining as many fibrous roots as possible in sizes and shapes as specified in the most recent edition of the *American Standard for Nursery Stock*. Balls shall be firmly wrapped with nonsynthetic, rottable burlap and secured with nails and heavy nonsynthetic, rottable twine. Root collar will be apparent at surface of ball. No trees with loose, broken, or manufactured balls will be planted, **except with special written approval before planting**.

C. Plants grown in containers shall be of appropriate size for the container as specified in the most recent edition of the *American Standard for Nursery Stock*, and be free of circling roots on the exterior and interior of the root ball.

D. All other types of nursery stock shall also conform to the *American Standard for Nursery Stock*.

XI. Transportation and Storage of Plant Material

(NOTE: No matter how good plant materials may be at a nursery, how that material is handled after it is dug is of critical importance.)

A. Fresh dug material is given preference over plant material held in storage. Plant material held in storage will be rejected if excessive growth or dieback of branches has occurred in storage.

B. Branches shall be tied with rope or twine only, and in such a manner that no damage will occur to the bark or branches.

C. During transportation of plant material, the Contractor shall exercise care to prevent injury and drying out of the trees. Should the roots be dried out, large branches broken, balls of earth broken or loosened, or areas of bark torn, the Owner's Representative may reject the injured tree(s) and order them replaced at no additional cost to the owner.

D. Each load of bare root stock sent from the storage facility shall be adequately covered with wet soil, sawdust, woodchips, moss, peat, straw, hay, or other acceptable moisture-holding medium, and shall be covered with a tarpaulin or canvas. Loads that are not protected in the above manner may be rejected.

E. Plants must be protected at all times from sun or drying winds. Those that cannot be planted immediately on delivery shall be kept in the shade, well protected with soil covered with wet wood chips or other acceptable material, and kept well watered. Plants shall not remain unplanted any longer than 3 days after delivery. Plants shall not be bound with wire or rope at any time so as to damage the bark or break branches. Plants shall be lifted and handled with suitable support of the soil ball to avoid damaging it.

XII. Mechanized Tree Spade Requirements

Trees may be moved and planted with an approved mechanical tree spade. The tree spade shall move trees limited to the maximum size allowed for a similar B&B root ball diameter according to the *American Standard for Nursery Stock*, or the manufacturer's maximum size recommendation for the tree spade being used, **whichever is smaller**. The machine shall be approved by the Owner's Representative prior to use. Trees shall be planted at the designated locations in the manner shown in the plans and in accordance with applicable sections of the specifications.

XIII.   Excavation of Planted Areas

A.   Locations for plants and outlines of areas to be planted are to be staked out at the site. Approval of the Owner's Representative is required before excavation begins. A minimum of 30 percent total planting must be staked out before inspection.

B.   Shrub beds are to be excavated to a depth of 1 ft (30 cm) unless otherwise indicated. Ground cover beds are to be excavated to a depth of 6 in (15 cm), unless otherwise indicated. Tree pits shall be excavated three times wider than the diameter of the ball, unless otherwise specified by the owners representative, and only as deep as the root ball to be placed in the hole. If initially dug too deep, the soil added to bring it up to the correct level should be thoroughly tamped. The sides of all plant holes shall be sloped and the bottoms horizontal. On slopes, the depth of the excavation shall be measured at the center of the hole. Poor quality subgrade soils shall be separated from the topsoil, removed from the area, and not used as backfill or otherwise spread around in the landscape area. Pits shall not be left uncovered or unprotected overnight.

C.   Detrimental soil conditions: The Owner's Representative is to be notified, in writing, of soil conditions that the Contractor considers detrimental to the growth of plant material. These conditions are to be described as well as suggestions for correcting them. Proper water drainage must be assured.

D.   Obstructions: If rock, underground construction work, tree roots, or obstructions are encountered in the excavation of plant pits, alternate locations may be selected by the Owner's Representative. Where locations cannot be changed as determined by the Owner's Representative, and where digging is permitted, submit cost required to remove the obstruction to a depth of not less than 6 in (15 cm) below the required hole depth. Proceed with work after approval of the Owner's Representative.

XIV.   Planting Operations

A.   Plants shall be set at the same relationship to finished grade as they were to the ground from which they were dug. Plants must be set plumb and braced in position until prepared topsoil has been placed around the ball and roots. Plants shall be set so that they will be the same depth 1 year later. The trunk of the tree is not to be used as a lever in positioning or moving the tree in the planting hole.

(NOTE: Because some nurseries practice tilling around trees, the root flare may be buried several inches deep. In some cases the top of the root ball may be at ground level, but the root flare actually is too deep. Proper planting depth requires the root flare to be at or slightly above the finished grade. It is *important to determine how deep the root flare is in the ball before it is placed in the planting hole. Sometimes the top of the ball may need to be raised until the root flare is at the proper planting depth. Remove the excess soil on the top of the root ball.)*

B. Ropes, strings, and wrapping from the top half of the root ball are to be removed after the plant has been set. All waterproof or water repellant wrappings shall be removed from the ball. Remove at least the top half of the wire basket before backfilling.

C. The roots of bare root trees shall be pruned at the time of planting to remove damaged or undesirable roots (those likely to become a detriment to future growth of the root system). Bare root trees shall have the roots spread to approximate the natural position of the roots and shall be centered in the planting pit. The planting soil backfill shall be worked firmly into and around the roots, with care taken to fill in completely with no air pockets.

D. When specified by the owner's representative, amend the backfill soil by adding 5 percent (by weight, 20-35 percent by volume, depending on materials) composted organic matter. In heavy clay soils use soil from the site, composted organic matter and sand in equal volumes.

E. Basins are to be formed around tree and shrub root ball with a raised ring of soil as indicated on drawing.

F. Planting areas are to be finish graded to conform to grades on drawing after full settlement has occurred.

G. Plants are to be thoroughly watered immediately after planting.

H. Any excess soil, debris, or trimmings shall be removed from the planting site immediately upon completion of each planting operation.

XV. Guying, Staking, Wrapping, Pruning, and Mulching

A. Stake trees only when necessary. Trees with light container soil balls and trees in windy areas are examples of situations that may require staking.

B. Staking and guying shall be completed immediately after planting. Trees up to 2 in (5 cm) caliper are to be staked with two stakes and separate flexible ties as shown on drawings. For larger trees, use 3 guy wires and ground anchors. Ground anchors are to be driven at approximately a 45-degree angle to ground plane and distributed at 120-degree intervals around the trunk. Anchors shall be driven to minimum vertical depth as follows:

Tree caliper		Anchor size		Minimum depth	
(in)	*(cm)*	*(in)*	*(cm)*	*(ft)*	*(m)*
2-5	5-13	4	10	2.0	0.6
5-7	13-18	6	15	3.5	1.0
>7	>18	8	20	4.0	1.2

Guying cables, turnbuckles, and hose are to be attached securely until the tree is well supported.

C. Guying and staking materials: Ground anchors shall be arrowhead shaped earth anchors of malleable iron castings, aluminum castings, or stamped steel. Staking wire shall be pliable 12-gauge galvanized, twisted two strands. Guying cable shall be 5 strand, 3/16 in (5 mm) diameter steel cable. Vertical supporting stakes shall be sound, uniform oak, redwood, or cedar. They shall be a minimum of 2 x 3 in (5 x 8 cm) in diameter, 8 ft (2.4 m) long, and pointed at one end. Hose shall be a suitable length of 2-ply reinforced, black rubber hose, 3/4 in (18 mm) in diameter.

D. If the use of tree wraps is specified by the Owner's Representative, wrapping materials shall be a standard manufactured tree wrapping paper, brown in color, with a crinkled surface. Trunks of deciduous trees 1.5 in (4 cm) or more caliper are to be wrapped with a spiral overlapping wrapping to a minimum height of the first branch. Trunks should be wrapped from the bottom to the top and fastened securely in place with paper tape. Stapling and the use of nylon tape or nylon string shall not be permitted. Wrapping shall be removed at the beginning of the second growing season.

E. Plants are to be pruned at the time of planting and according to best horticulture practice. Pruning of all trees will include the removal of injured branches, double leaders, watersprouts, suckers, and interfering limbs. Healthy lower branches and small twigs close to the center should not be removed, except as necessary to clear sidewalks or streets. All pruning cuts shall be clean and smooth, with the bark intact and uninjured at the edges. In no case shall more than one-third of the branching structure be removed, **leaving the normal shape of the plant in tact**. If use of tree paint is specified by the Owner's Representative, it shall be a standard type specifically recommended as tree wound dressing paint.

F. All trees, shrubs, and other planting beds will be mulched with a mixture of shredded wood and bark previously approved by the owner. The composted mulch will be free of materials injurious to plant growth, branches, leaves, roots, and other extraneous matter. The mulch will be 2 to 4 in (5 to 10 cm) deep on trees and shrubs. The depth of mulch on other planting beds will be _____ in. Mulch must not be placed within 3 in (8 cm) of the trunks of trees or shrubs.

G. Antitranspirant when used shall be an emulsion that provides a protective film over plant surfaces and is nontoxic to all plants used. It shall be delivered in containers of the manufacturer and mixed according to the manufacturer's directions.

XVI. Maintenance of Trees, Shrubs, and Vines

A. Maintenance shall begin immediately after each plant is planted and continue until its acceptance has been confirmed by the Owner's Representative.

B. Maintenance shall consist of pruning, watering, cultivating, weeding, mulching, tightening and repairing guys and stakes, resetting plants to proper grades or upright position, restoration of the planting saucer, and furnishing and applying such sprays or other materials as are necessary to keep plantings free of insects and diseases and in vigorous condition.

C. Planting areas and plants shall be protected at all times against trespassing and damage of all kinds for the duration of the maintenance period. If a plant becomes damaged or injured, it shall be treated or replaced as directed by the Owner's Representative at no additional cost.

D. Watering: Contractor shall irrigate, as required, to maintain vigorous and healthy tree growth. Over-watering or flooding shall not be allowed. Contractor shall use existing irrigation facilities and furnish any additional material, equipment, or water to ensure adequate irrigation. During periods of restricted water usage, all governmental regulations (permanent and temporary) shall be followed. Should modifications of existing irrigation systems and/or schedules facilitate adherence to these regulations, the Contractor shall notify the owner of the suggested modifications. The Contractor may have to transport water from ponds or other sources when irrigation systems are unavailable.

XVII. **Acceptance**

The Owner's Representative shall inspect all work for acceptance upon written request of the Contractor. The request shall be received at least 10 calendar days before the anticipated date of inspection.

Acceptance of plant material by the Owner's Representative shall be for general conformance to specified size, character, and quality and shall not relieve the Contractor of responsibility for full conformance to the contract documents, including correct species.

Upon completion and reinspection of all repairs or renewals necessary in the judgment of the Owner's Representative, the Owner's Representative shall certify in writing that the work has been accepted.

XVIII. **Acceptance in Part**

Work may be accepted in parts when the Owner's Representative and Contractor deem that practice to be in their mutual interest. Approval must be given in writing by the Owner's Representative to the Contractor verifying that the work is to be completed in parts. Acceptance of work in parts shall not waive any other provision of this contract.

XIX. **Guarantee Period and Replacements**

A. The guarantee period for trees and shrubs shall begin at the date of acceptance.

B. The Contractor shall guarantee all plant material to be in healthy and flourishing condition for a period of 1 year from the date of acceptance.

C. When work is accepted in parts, the guarantee periods extend from each of the partial acceptances to the terminal date of the guarantee of the last acceptance. Thus, all guarantee periods terminate at one time.

D. The Contractor shall replace, without cost, as soon as weather conditions permit, and within a specified planting period, all plants determined by the Owner's Representative to be dead or in an unacceptable condition during and at the end of the guarantee period. To be considered acceptable, plants shall be free of dead or dying branches and branch tips and shall bear foliage of normal density, size, and color. Replacements shall closely match adjacent specimens of the same species. Replacements shall be subject to all requirements stated in this specification.

E. The guarantee of all replacement plants shall extend for an additional period of 1 year from the date of their acceptance after replacement. In the event that a replacement plant is not acceptable during or at the end of the said extended guarantee period, the Owner's Representative may elect subsequent replacement or credit for that item.

F. The Contractor shall make periodic inspections, at no extra cost, during the guarantee period to determine what changes, if any, should be made in the maintenance program. If changes are recommended, they shall be submitted in writing to the Owner's Representative.

XX. Final Inspection and Final Acceptance

(NOTE: Inspections may be made before, during, and after planting trees and shrubs. Some Owners prefer to inspect and select nursery stock at the nursery. Others inspect it upon arrival or at planting time. It is best to reject trees before they are planted. Inspection of the work site should occur during the first day of planting to insure that the Contractor understands the specifications. In addition to an inspection after the work is completed, occasional inspection should be conducted as the work progresses. The final inspection occurs at the end of the guarantee period. At this time, decisions are made whether more trees are to be replaced.)

At the end of the guarantee period and upon written request of the Contractor, the Owner's Representative will inspect all guaranteed work for final acceptance. The request shall be received at least 10 calendar days before the anticipated date for final inspection. Upon completion and reinspection of all repairs or renewals necessary in the judgment of the Owner's Representative at that time, the Owner's Representative shall certify, in writing, that the project has received final acceptance.

XXI. Payment

(NOTE: The basis for payment to the Contractor may be included in the General Provisions section or in this section.)

Payment shall be made to the Contractor as follows:

(Example)

- 50% of contract sum upon receipt and approval of plant materials by the owner.
- 35% of the contract sum upon completion of planting of the plant materials.
- 10% of contract sum after the replanting of replacement material if required.
- 5% of contract sum after final acceptance.

XXII. Planting Diagram

(NOTE: Diagram of a typical planting site. Some sites will require special modifications.)

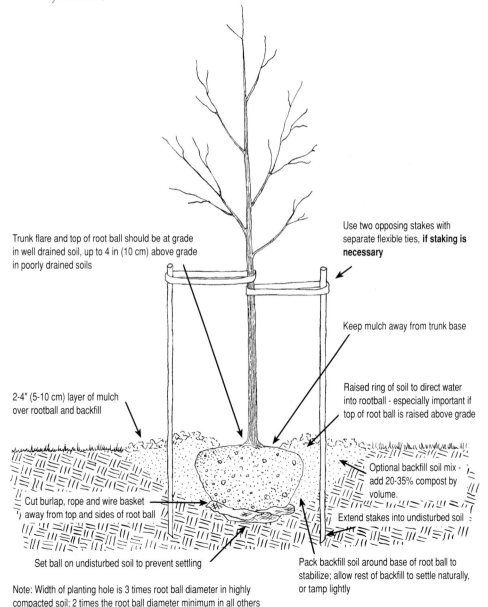

Use two opposing stakes with separate flexible ties, **if staking is necessary**

Trunk flare and top of root ball should be at grade in well drained soil, up to 4 in (10 cm) above grade in poorly drained soils

Keep mulch away from trunk base

2-4" (5-10 cm) layer of mulch over rootball and backfill

Raised ring of soil to direct water into rootball - especially important if top of root ball is raised above grade

Optional backfill soil mix - add 20-35% compost by volume.

Cut burlap, rope and wire basket away from top and sides of root ball

Extend stakes into undisturbed soil

Set ball on undisturbed soil to prevent settling

Pack backfill soil around base of root ball to stabilize; allow rest of backfill to settle naturally, or tamp lightly

Note: Width of planting hole is 3 times root ball diameter in highly compacted soil; 2 times the root ball diameter minimum in all others

Gary Watson is a member of the research staff at the Morton Arboretum working on root development of trees in urban landscapes. The primary focus of his research is understanding how to control the balance between the crown and the root system for healthier trees. This has lead to studies on construction injury, soil improvements and mulching, root development after transplanting, mycorrhizae, root pruning, girdling roots, fertilization, and plant growth regulators. He is co-editor of two other ISA publications, **The Landscape Below Ground** and **Trees & Building Sites**. He has served as President of the Illinois Chapter of ISA and the Arboricultural Research and Education Academy. He was elected Vice President of ISA in 1997.

E. B. Himelick retired in 1988 as Professor Emeritus from both the University of Illinois and the Natural History Survey, Urbana, Illinois. He was a Plant Pathologist doing field research on both forest and urban tree diseases for 36 years. He served for 10 years as Executive Director of The International Society of Arboriculture and is presently Research Associate to The Morton Arboretum. Himelick has been a national consultant on urban tree disease diagnosis and tree problems for 45 years. Primary areas of applied field research were on control of the vascular tree diseases Dutch elm disease and oak wilt and on transplanting, fertilization, and chlorosis of urban trees. Over 300 research and educational publications have been published during his professional career.